Looking around the room at his teammates, LeBron asked, "What's my excuse now?"

"I've got all of you on this team. So, what's my excuse now?" His words built momentum as he spoke. "This is everything we've always dreamed of, having that guy next to you and winning something. That gold medal is what we've all been dreaming about. I'm excited. And I know you guys are. This is what I've always wanted, playing alongside Carmelo, playing alongside Jason, and playing with Kobe. We don't have an excuse now. None of us."
                    —from THE GOLD STANDARD

"Fascinating."
 —The Wall Street Journal Report with Maria Bartiromo,
                    CNBC

"Very dramatic . . . a highly enjoyable and revealing behind-the-scenes read . . . The broad messages will be valuable to all."
                    —Toronto Globe and Mail

ALSO BY MIKE KRZYZEWSKI

Beyond Basketball
Five-Point Play
Leading with the Heart

The Gold Standard

Standard

Building a World-Class Team

MIKE KRZYZEWSKI
WITH JAMIE K. SPATOLA

GRAND CENTRAL
PUBLISHING

NEW YORK   BOSTON

Grand Central Publishing
Hachette Book Group
1290 Avenue of the Americas
New York, NY 10104
www.HachetteBookGroup.com

Grand Central Publishing is a division of Hachette Book Group, Inc.
The Grand Central Publishing name and logo are trademarks of
Hachette Book Group, Inc..

Originally published in hardcover by Hachette Book Group

Printed in the United States of America

First Trade Edition: April 2010

10 9 8 7 6

The Hachette Speakers Bureau provides a wide range of authors for speaking
events. To find out more, go to www.hachettespeakersbureau.com
or call (866) 376-6591.

The publisher is not responsible for websites (or their content)
that are not owned by the publisher.

The Library of Congress has cataloged the hardcover edition as follows:
Krzyzewski, Mike.
   The gold standard : building a world-class team / Mike Krzyzewski with Jamie
K. Spatola. — 1st ed.
      p. cm.
   ISBN 978-0-446-54407-8
   1. Basketball teams—United States.   2. Olympic Games (29th : 2008 : Beijing,
China)   3. Teamwork (Sports)   I. Spatola, Jamie K.   II. Title.

   GV885.7.K79   2009
   796.323092—dc22
                            2009001161
ISBN 978-0-446-54406-1 (pbk.)

Book design by Charles Sutherland

Dedicated to our military men and women,
who taught us the meaning of selfless service

CONTENTS

PREFACE

With eight minutes and twenty-three seconds left in the gold-medal basketball game of the 2008 Olympics, I called a timeout. Our United States team led Spain by only two points: 91–89.

Pressure-filled moments like this one are about who your team has become. You hope you have developed a great shared character. You may even think that you have. But you don't *know* until this moment. This is the time when it's tested.

We had been together through enough time and competition to truly become a team. And now we had to trust that the relationships we had formed, the standards we had established, and the practice in which we had engaged had made us worthy of winning. There is a time to call a play and a time to let them play. It was time to let them play.

THE GOLD STANDARD CHRONOLOGY

2005

April 27, 2005	Jerry Colangelo named managing director for USA Basketball
June 5, 2005	Jerry Colangelo hosts conference with former Olympic players and coaches in Chicago
July 22, 2005	Jerry Colangelo and Mike Krzyzewski discuss national coach position in Las Vegas
October 26, 2005	Mike Krzyzewski named national coach
December 2005	Jerry Colangelo begins interviews to find National Team players

2006

May 6–7, 2006	USAB coaching staff gathers for the first time in Phoenix
July 18, 2006	Players arrive for training camp in Las Vegas
July 25, 2006	Training camp breaks
July 31, 2006	Training camp resumes
August 3, 2006	USA exhibition versus Puerto Rico in Las Vegas (W, 114–69)
August 4–5, 2006	Team travels to Guangzhou, China

August 7, 2006   USA exhibition versus China in Guangzhou
                        (W, 119–73)

August 9, 2006   USA exhibition versus Brazil in Guangzhou
                        (W, 90–86)

August 11, 2006   Team travels to Seoul, South Korea

August 13, 2006   USA exhibition versus Lithuania in Seoul
                        (W, 111–88)

August 14, 2006   Visit and practice at Yongsan Army Garrison in
                        South Korea

August 15, 2006   USA exhibition versus South Korea in Seoul
                        (W, 116–63)

August 16, 2006   Visit and practice at Camp Casey military base
                        in South Korea

August 17, 2006   Team travels to Sapporo, Japan

August 19, 2006   USA versus Puerto Rico in FIBA World Champi-
                        onship pool play
                        (W, 111–100)

August 20, 2006   USA versus China in FIBA World Championship
                        pool play
                        (W, 121–90)

August 22, 2006   USA versus Slovenia in FIBA World Champion-
                        ship pool play
                        (W, 114–95)

August 23, 2006   USA versus Italy in FIBA World Championship
                        pool play
                        (W, 94–85)

August 24, 2006   USA versus Senegal in FIBA World Champion-
                        ship pool play
                        (W, 103–58)

August 25, 2006	Team travels to Tokyo, Japan
August 27, 2006	USA versus Australia in FIBA World Championship Eighth-Finals (W, 113–73)
August 28, 2006	Visit to Yokosuka Naval Base
August 29, 2006	USA versus Germany in FIBA World Championship Quarterfinals (W, 85–65)
September 1, 2006	USA versus Greece in FIBA World Championship Semifinals (L, 95–101)
September 2, 2006	USA versus Argentina in FIBA World Championship bronze-medal game (W, 96–81)
September 4, 2006	Team travels back to the United States

2007

April 23, 2007	USAB coaching staff meeting in Phoenix
July 19, 2007	Players arrive for mini-camp in Las Vegas
July 20–21, 2007	Daily team practices
July 22, 2007	Blue/White National Team inter-squad exhibition in Las Vegas
July 23, 2007	Mini-camp breaks
August 14, 2007	Players arrive for training camp in Las Vegas
August 14–21, 2007	Daily practices in Las Vegas

August 22, 2007	USA versus Venezuela in FIBA Americas Championship pool play (W, 112–69)
August 23, 2007	USA versus US Virgin Islands in FIBA Americas Championship pool play (W, 123–59)
August 25, 2007	USA versus Canada in FIBA Americas Championship pool play (W, 113–63)
August 26, 2007	USA versus Brazil in FIBA Americas Championship pool play (W, 113–76)
August 27, 2007	USA versus Mexico in FIBA Americas Championship Second Round (W, 127–100)
August 28, 2007	USA versus Puerto Rico in FIBA Americas Championship Second Round (W, 117–78)
August 29, 2007	USA versus Uruguay in FIBA Americas Championship Second Round (W, 118–79)
August 30, 2007	USA versus Argentina in FIBA Americas Championship Second Round (W, 91–76)
September 1, 2007	USA versus Puerto Rico in FIBA Americas Championship Semifinals (W, 135–91)
September 2, 2007	USA versus Argentina in FIBA Americas Championship Finals (W, 118–81)

2008

April 28, 2008	USAB coaching staff meeting in Phoenix
June 22, 2008	2008 Olympic team announcement in Chicago
June 27, 2008	Players arrive for mini-camp in Las Vegas
June 28, 2008	First Olympic team practice
June 29, 2008	Team travels to New York City
June 30, 2008	Team PR appearances and pep rally in Rockefeller Center
July 20, 2008	Players arrive for training camp in Las Vegas
July 21–24, 2008	Daily team practices
July 25, 2008	USA exhibition versus Canada in Las Vegas (W, 120–65)
July 26, 2008	Team travels to Macau, China
July 29–30, 2008	Daily team practices in Macau
July 31, 2008	USA exhibition versus Turkey in Macau (W, 114–82)
August 1, 2008	USA exhibition versus Lithuania in Macau (W, 120–84)
August 2, 2008	Team travels to Shanghai, China
August 3, 2008	USA exhibition versus Russia in Shanghai (W, 89–68)
August 5, 2008	USA exhibition versus Australia in Shanghai (W, 87–76)
August 6, 2008	Team travels to Beijing

THE GOLD STANDARD CHRONOLOGY

August 7–9, 2008	Daily team practices
August 8, 2008	2008 Olympic Games Opening Ceremonies
August 10, 2008	USA versus China in Olympic pool play (W, 101–70)
August 12, 2008	USA versus Angola in Olympic pool play (W, 97–76)
August 14, 2008	USA versus Greece in Olympic pool play (W, 92–69)
August 16, 2008	USA versus Spain in Olympic pool play (W, 119–82)
August 18, 2008	USA versus Germany in Olympic pool play (W, 106–57)
August 20, 2008	USA versus Australia in Olympic Quarterfinals (W, 116–85)
August 22, 2008	USA versus Argentina in Olympic Semifinals (W, 101–81)
August 24, 2008	USA versus Spain in Olympic gold-medal game (W, 118–107)
August 25, 2008	Team travels back to the United States
November 12, 2008	Jerry Colangelo named chairman of the USA Basketball board of directors for 2009–2012

INTRODUCTION:
TEAM BUILDING IN TIME AND MOMENTS

Because I have been a coach for the majority of my life, I am often asked, "How do you build a team?" This book is my response to that question. My proudest times as a coach are those when I recognize that a group of players has become a team, a whole that is truly greater than the sum of its parts. From the summer of 2006 through the 2008 Summer Olympics in Beijing, I had the opportunity to work with a group whose parts were some of the most talented basketball players in the game. And I had the privilege of being their coach as this amazing team came together to bring the gold medal back to the United States. In serving as the national coach for USA Basketball over this three-year period, I was lucky enough to have the most gratifying experience of my career. It was an experience that I believe illustrates what team building is all about.

You do not select a team, you select a group of people and then work together to develop into a team. In other words, teams don't instantaneously *become*, they *evolve*. To do so, you need *time*, *goals*, and *competition*.

When I say "time," I don't simply mean the amount of days, hours, or weeks that you spend with one another, though this quantity of time is vitally important. I really mean the way you spend that time. I mean the quality of it, the focus. When you are given the responsibility of building a team, you must make time for certain things. Time to form relationships. Time to establish standards. Time to get motivated. In the same vein, there are certain things for which there is no time. No time for excuses. No time for surprises. No time for inner turmoil. Leaders are responsible for ensuring that you spend both the necessary quantity and quality of time to get the job done and for making certain that no time is wasted.

Every team needs an ultimate goal, a purpose for which it unites and prepares. Thinking about the goal that lies ahead is what gives your team energy. It's what you get excited about. It's why you practice hard. No matter what intermediate steps you take, your team should always have your ultimate goal in mind and allow its pursuit to invigorate you.

Competition is also vital to success in team building. In some cases, competition may be the very reason you have a team. But regardless of your goal, the competition your team will encounter must inform your decisions as a leader. You must develop a comprehensive understanding of who and what you're facing. Your training and preparation are then based on this understanding.

Throughout the course of your team's life span, competition also serves as an opportunity for self-assessment. How your team functions under the pressure of competition can help the leader judge the effectiveness of your training, determine the direction you need to take, and discover what changes and improvements must be made. You train, you go to combat, and then you *re*train—it's how you ensure that you are evolving the right way.

The single most important decision USA Basketball made was selecting Jerry Colangelo as its managing director. No more committees. No more throwing teams together just weeks before Olympic competition. Jerry became a one-man committee who would give USA Basketball the essential gift of time, and he would insist that we devote much of that time to a fuller understanding of our competition and our ultimate goal. By instilling a program as opposed to an ad-hoc team, Jerry asked for an unprecedented three-year commitment from coaches and athletes.

When approached to be the first head coach under the new National Team concept, I readily accepted this commitment. In fact, I didn't even think about it; I instinctively accepted. I understood the need for a new methodology. I, too, had watched as the United States had lost its competitive edge in international basketball. This is not to place blame on those involved with the 2004 Olympic basketball team, a team that was comprised of some of the most talented players and some of the most knowledgeable coaches in the game. In my perspective, the system failed them. That team was sent into competition ill-prepared. It was not a lack of talent or basketball know-how; it was simply a lack of the proper time and competition. Thanks to Jerry, we were given that time. Then it was up to us, together, to ensure that it was time well spent.

People want a recipe; they want a formula for how to build a team that will serve its intended purpose. Recipes guarantee that if you follow these steps and in this order, you will get a favorable outcome. But team building is *not* about a recipe, it's about taking the necessary time to build *this* team for *this* purpose.

Many have said that I coached the Olympic team differently than I coach my Duke teams. Of course I did. If I'm doing my job right, I also coach my Duke teams differently each season. Your team-building plan must be personalized and specific to your personnel, your competition, your goal, and your leadership style. I can't just give you a formula. But I can offer you my thoughts on how to best utilize your time in bringing a team together. You have to be willing to invest the time in preparation, to figure it out and to personalize it. And that's what makes it interesting.

The time you spend as a team is defined by moments: moments that unite, create understanding, and allow you to discover your collective identity. These moments make you one, make you better, make you proud. Some moments are planned. You know they need to happen, so you design them. But there are other moments that happen on their own, a natural by-product of team formation. Still other moments pass by unnoticed until you discover their importance later on. You come to realize what they really meant and how critical they actually were.

How do you build a team? Embrace moments. Plan for moments. There are moments of anger, moments of joy, moments of togetherness, and sometimes just moments of awareness. Learn how to recognize them, facilitate them, reevaluate them, and, most important, share them. They are the lifeblood of your team.

As I look back over the three years I spent as the national coach, I feel extreme pride. I will never forget the looks on the faces of my team as they stood together on the medal stand in Beijing and had gold medals placed around their necks. Carmelo Anthony with an American flag draped over his shoulders. Kobe Bryant and Chris Bosh singing along as our national anthem played. LeBron James's strong, dignified look as he placed his hand over his heart. Tears in Dwyane Wade's eyes.

I am proud of the players and of my fellow coaches for what they all brought to this endeavor. Of course, I am proud that we won and that we won in a manner that represented both our sport and our country well. But what I am most proud of is the fact that I was a part of a remarkable *team*, one that shared some unforgettable moments.

This book is divided into times and moments, with each chapter devoted to a particular quality of time I feel is vital to team building. These "times" are presented in an order that was chosen purposefully, but that does not mean that you can simply do one thing, check it off the list, and be done with it. Team building is an ongoing process, and, in a way, all of these "times" should be happening together throughout your team's life span. Within each chapter, I have also included some of the moments that defined that time for us as the USA Basketball Men's Senior National Team.

Because we spent this time and because we shared these moments, this team will be bonded for life. In coming together, we gave of ourselves to become something bigger than all of us: a world-class team.

TIME TO CHOOSE YOUR PEOPLE

When deciding which individuals to select to form a team, you have to ask the hard questions. This requires a look back at what has been done before and why it may or may not have worked. Often the difficulty lay not in finding the answers but in asking the questions. In making decisions about our team, it was the first step.

The most difficult questions to ask are usually the most basic: the whos, whats, whens, wheres, and, most important, the whys and the hows. Your particular task and specific set of challenges will lend more specificity to these questions. Jerry and I prepared the list below.

- Who
    o   are we playing against?
    o   will we bring together to face that competition?
    o   do we represent?
- What
    o   are our particular challenges?
    o   was missing in our recent losses?
    o   is our motivation?

- When
  - o   are we playing?
  - o   do we assemble to grow together as a unit?
- Where
  - o   are we playing?
  - o   is our venue and what particular challenges does it present?
- Why
  - o   was the old system not working?
  - o   do we care?
- How
  - o   do we change a culture?
  - o   do we prepare to meet our challenge?
  - o   much time do we have to prepare?

No doubt, the root answers to all of these questions lay in the analysis of where we had gone wrong. What could we learn from the past? The basic message was clear, and I think Jerry Colangelo said it best: "Guys who play *together* can beat a group of all-stars on any given night." Team over talent. Collective identity over individual ego. And so we looked to those teams that had been successful, that had been achieving as we fell behind. We borrowed from international teams like Argentina and Spain the need for familiarity with one another and for continuity.

In asking for a three-year commitment from the pool of thirty-three American players with whom he spoke, Jerry gave the USA Basketball program that continuity. It was easy to point fingers and blame this guy or that guy for the way he acted or didn't act in 2004, but Jerry and I both believed that it was our current system that was flawed, not the players. This system was no longer conducive to winning. I eagerly signed up to be a part of the program. I like the way Coach Mike D'Antoni, one of the three National Team assistant coaches, put it when he said, "You need to keep guys together, have them make a commitment. It doesn't guarantee success, but it guarantees you a chance." Thanks to our new system, we definitely had a chance, one that was not given to the 2004 team.

In assembling a team that would represent our country in basketball over the next three years, obviously it was important to evaluate what we might have been missing on the court in years past. In this regard, there are certain personnel components that I believe will make any team better, in basketball or business.

For one thing, there is no substitute for talent. And while a great attitude and a solid game plan will take you far, you cannot achieve at the highest level without having some aptitude. At Duke, I used to run good plays for Grant Hill. But then Grant Hill graduated, and all of a sudden those weren't good plays anymore. You need the talent to fill out your system. Fortunately for our US team, talent was never a problem. The pool from which we had to choose included the elite, professional basketball players of the United States.

I also believe that a team needs some people with experience—veterans. Often those who have been in a particular business the longest are ignored, their contributions replaced by those of the newest up-and-comer. But it's the veterans who have the deepest level of institutional understanding and who can pass this experience on to the other members of your team. The veterans are also those who grasp the concept of legacy. Legacy asks the question, "Who were you? Did you win? Did you lose? Did you do something special?" Trust me, the people who are experienced enough to ask these questions can motivate your team.

Don't get me wrong, I'm not saying that your group doesn't need a youthful element. It absolutely does. Youth brings a certain excitement to your undertaking that helps keep the team and you, as the leader, fresh. That's one thing I have appreciated about being in coaching for so long: being around youthful energy has helped keep me feeling young. Youthful enthusiasm is an essential element for any team.

For the basketball part of it, we had to find a group that could work together offensively. But, more important, we had to select people who could come together and become one solid force on the defensive end of the court. In a business setting and, of course, depending on your goal, the best team for a particular job may be the one that can write and execute the best business plan, or the one that can generate the most creative marketing ideas. But in the basketball business, I have always felt that a great team is the one that can be unified on the defensive end of the floor. What are the core competencies that your team needs to accomplish your goal? The answer to this question will assist you in choosing the people your organization needs to go forward.

Personalities are also a factor. When I was named the national coach in 2005, I made a promise that Jerry and I would put together a team of players who would represent us well both on and off the court. So, who would be the group of men willing to give of themselves to become a part of something bigger? What group of players would be willing to buy in to the three-year commitment and new National Team concept? As it turned out, earning a commitment from the players who joined our team was a lot easier than I had anticipated.

Carmelo Anthony, Carlos Boozer, LeBron James, and Dwyane Wade were ready to sign up again as soon as they stepped off the bronze-medal stand in 2004, the last time they had worn red, white, and blue. They knew—like Jerry—that USA Basketball needed to be turned upside down. And those who watched from afar as we lost three games in 2004 Olympic play were just as ready to redefine USA Basketball as those who had participated.

Moment: Dinner with Jerry Colangelo—July 22, 2005—Las Vegas, Nevada

In embarking on a discussion of how this team was selected, I would be remiss not to mention my own selection as head coach and not to credit Jerry with his blueprint for this team—this program—from its outset. The incredible bond that Jerry and I have was cemented at my favorite restaurant, Michael's, in Las Vegas over a dinner the two of us shared in July 2005.

The meeting was set up the previous week when Jerry called me at home. I knew he had been brought on as managing director for USA Basketball, and I knew he had been talking to former Olympians and coaches in asking those hard questions and studying what changes needed to be made. Having worked with USA Basketball in one way or another since 1979, I wasn't surprised to hear from Jerry. But I never thought that I would be his choice for head coach; I believed that my time to head up an Olympic team had passed when they began using professional players in 1992. No way would anyone bring in a college coach to lead professional superstars. Some of the guys on the team had never even played for a college coach, having chosen to go directly from high school to the NBA. In that first phone call, Jerry was gleaning my interest and, even after a long talk, he told me that there was more for us to discuss. Since I was scheduled to be in Las Vegas for recruiting the next week and Jerry was to be there on business, we agreed to meet for dinner.

It was a great evening. The décor at Michael's is a throwback to the dining rooms of old Vegas: red velvet chairs, crystal chandeliers, and a stained-glass skylight overhead, producing an elegant and nostalgic atmosphere. It's the type of place where a three-hour dinner is not uncommon and, no matter how long you've stayed, you always hate to leave. Over the years, my family and I have shared some special moments at Michael's. This night became one to add to the list.

At one point during dinner, I asked Jerry about his taking on the substantial responsibility of directing the reconstruction of USA Men's Basketball. "You've already done so much in your career," I said, "and this is a risky undertaking. Why did you decide to do it?"

I will never forget his response. "Because I love the game and the game's been good to me," he told me. "We owe the game."

And he was right. The game had been good to both of us—so good, in fact, that we could never fully repay it.

I'll also never forget how I felt when Jerry told me that the position of national coach was mine for the taking. He described to me his vision for the next Olympic team, how he planned to completely turn the culture of USA Basketball around, and how he felt that I was the guy to help him do it. I knew that I needed to go home and discuss this major, life-changing decision with my wife and family, but I was compelled to accept immediately even before talking it over with the people I love most.

Of course, there are anxieties that come along with an undertaking like this one. But I can honestly say that they did not enter my mind in the moment of my acceptance. When I got back to my home in Durham, we had a family get-together to discuss the position, the challenges that came with it, and how it would all affect us. It was at that gathering that those underlying anxieties first began to surface.

"How are you going to make the time in your schedule to do this for three summers?" my wife asked.

"Can you promise us that it won't wear you down too much and that you will stay healthy?" my daughter Lindy said.

My daughter Debbie raised the question, "Do you think professional players will listen to you the same way your Duke players do?"

And, of course, there was talking all around the question that everyone had in mind but no one could muster the words to articulate: "What if we lose?"

I did not want to hear any of it. Naturally those questions were in my mind, too, but I refused to dwell on them. I didn't want to touch the feelings of apprehension that questions like those tend to bring about. It was frustrating for my family that I didn't have solid responses that night. But throughout the entire process, when the numerous questions arose, rarely did I know immediately how they would be answered. I just felt confident that the answers were there and that we would find them.

Jerry and I had known each other for many years but had operated in different worlds. We had both devoted our lives to sport, he on the professional level and I on the collegiate level. I had always had great respect for his accomplishments, but that night at Michael's there was an immediate and very special connection, one rooted in both a love of the game and a love of our country. We had both grown up in Chicago in Midwestern, ethnic, working-class surroundings. We both held a firm belief in the values instilled in us by our immigrant families. We came to discover how much we really had in common. Jerry said, "There must be something in the Chicago water." Whatever it was, from that moment on, Jerry Colangelo and I would be joined at the hip.

On October 26, 2005, Jerry and I appeared together in New York City, along with the 1992 Olympic "Dream Team" Head Coach Chuck Daly and USA Basketball President Val Ackerman, for a press conference officially naming me as the national coach. After Val's introduction, Jerry made his statement to the media. "When I was asked to take on the responsibility, I looked at it and said that it would be very challenging," he said. "I knew I would be passionate about it and it was going to be important to surround myself with people who felt exactly the same way. From the get-go, when I first met with Coach K, it was pretty evident where he stood, where his passion was, and how committed he would be if he were offered the job. When it came right down to it, and I had to make a choice, this was the guy—right time, right place—this was the guy I wanted alongside me to go forward." Leadership can be lonely. But I believe you can fight that loneliness by finding kindred spirits and surrounding yourself with those people who will bring out the best in you. Jerry and I provided that for one another.

Next, it was my turn to address the press. It was one of the proudest moments of my life. "For a coach, this is the ultimate honor, to have the opportunity to coach your country's team," I said. "I'm a guy who's always gotten into commitments. I had a four-year commitment to attend West Point and a five-year commitment to serve in the Army when I graduated. And that turned out pretty well. I have a commitment to my wife that has gone on for thirty-six years. That's turning out pretty well too. And so a three-year commitment doesn't seem like much. I love the game and I love the game at every level."

I went on to express my thanks, first, to the man who had been my coach at West Point, Bob Knight. Coach Knight had also given me my first opportunity with USA Basketball as his assistant coach in the 1979 Pan-American games. "Coach Knight has been like a father to me and a great friend," I said. "I called him last night and thanked him for what he's done for me in just getting me involved." I also thanked Chuck Daly, one of the great coaches from whom I had learned so much as one of his assistants on the 1992 Olympic team. "I thought that would be my ultimate Olympic experience," I said, "and it was a pretty darn good one." But now I had the chance to be the head coach of a United States team. What an honor. What an opportunity.

Jerry said that day and many times after that I was "the right guy at the right time." More than that, I believe that the relationship Jerry and I formed and our shared vision created the right partnership at the right time. With this relationship as our basis, I knew that our team was going in a great direction.

Moment: Jerry Colangelo Interviews Michael Redd— December 7, 2005—Chicago, Illinois

When building a team, the members of that team need to be explicitly told what the parameters of their commitment are going to be, what is expected of them. *The honesty and openness of your initial communication with these individuals lays the groundwork for the future of your relationship.* In team building, you want this foundation to be one of trust and forthright communication. There shouldn't be any surprises. It sounds like such a simple notion, but it's just not always done this way.

In figuring out which players would best represent USA Basketball, Jerry's approach was extremely businesslike. Businesslike and old-school. He spoke to each individual face-to-face and made certain that they understood exactly what his expectations were. In business, this would be done during the hiring process. In our case, the need for a cultural overhaul meant changing the way we do business. Jerry, the top guy in our organization, took the extensive amount of time that was needed and conducted the interviews personally. That was a key first step.

Jerry did not look to precedent to guide the way he conducted these interviews, because there simply was no precedent for what we were trying to accomplish. We were starting from scratch. As such, we wanted to select those individuals who had talent but who also had high standards. Jason Kidd, one of the key members of our 2007 and 2008 National Team rosters, was asked in an interview with Charlie Rose how a group of rich, talented NBA players with big egos came together to form this team. "From day one we set a tone," he said. "We respected what each other had done but the bottom line was the desire to win." In choosing our people, we sought out individuals with a standard of excellence. We had to be on common ground with these players, and we had to be sure that we could operate with a common purpose.

Jerry told me about his interviews as he conducted them. The reactions of all the players were impressive and exciting, but his interview with Michael Redd stood out. Michael had driven straight from his team practice in Milwaukee—where he was a starter averaging more than 20 points a game for his Milwaukee Bucks team—to meet with Jerry in Chicago. When Jerry answered the knock at his door, Michael was standing there in his warm-ups with a garment bag over his shoulder. After shaking Jerry's hand, Michael asked if he could be excused to the restroom. When he emerged a few minutes later, he was dressed in a suit and tie. "Okay, I'm ready now," he told Jerry.

I love that story. It is a terrific example of a feeling that had begun to grow among the NBA players who Jerry approached, a feeling that this would be significant. The players had begun to treat the process with the utmost respect and dignity. Michael showed that in the way he dressed for the job he wanted.

In his meetings with the players, Jerry began by talking a little about his own life, about growing up in a working-class Chicago family whose home was fashioned from an old railroad boxcar. He told them about his admiration for the grandparents who had come to this country in search of a better life for their future generations, and about the opportunities that sport had given him. Jerry told them of his sincere love for both the sport of basketball and for America, and the debt of gratitude he owed to each. He told them how he would put his legacy on the line in an attempt to repay this debt. He told them all of this and he asked them to do the same.

Of course, in speaking of the element of sacrifice involved, Jerry also told the players about the reward they could receive, making them all aware of the return they could get on their investment. But this compensation would not be monetary. No Olympic player or coach is paid for participation in the Olympics. Instead, their reward would come from regaining the respect of the international basketball community and reestablishing the gold standard for the future of USA Basketball. From the start, as Jerry describes it, "there was total buy-in. And it snowballed from there." In our conversations, Jerry and I talked often about how rewarding it was to see playing for your country once again become the "in thing."

Moment: Press Conference Announcing the 2008 Olympic Team—June 23, 2008—Chicago, Illinois

On June 23, 2008, it finally came time to announce our twelve-man Olympic roster. Jerry Colangelo, Carmelo Anthony, Dwyane Wade, and I gathered in Chicago for the occasion. In front of a room full of media Jerry announced, "The twelve players chosen for the *honor* of representing the United States in the 2008 Beijing Olympic games are: Carmelo Anthony, Carlos Boozer, Chris Bosh, Kobe Bryant, Dwight Howard, LeBron James, Jason Kidd, Chris Paul, Tayshaun Prince, Michael Redd, Dwyane Wade, and Deron Williams."

Carmelo would bring his scoring ability, his love of the game, and his million-dollar smile. I coached Carlos at Duke, so I already knew that he was the ultimate team player who had experience and great physical attributes. Chris Bosh would bring a defensive presence underneath the basket and would be an extremely versatile center ideally suited for the international game. Kobe had been the NBA's Most Valuable Player that season, so he clearly brought with him unmatched talent along with his love for being in pressure situations. Dwight's contribution would come through his tremendous strength and physical presence. And, who wouldn't choose LeBron? His combination of talent and charisma made him someone who would be a benefit to any basketball team. Jason would come to the team already a seasoned leader with unsurpassed knowledge of the game. Chris Paul, who was second in the running for league MVP, brought both playmaking and personality. Tayshaun had a willingness to accept any role on a team and the coinciding ability to be outstanding in that role. Michael was a man of great character and would contribute his deft shooting touch to our offensive arsenal. Dwyane was creative and explosive on both the offensive and defensive ends of the floor and also had a heart committed to the game. And Deron brought with him great courage on the court, the willingness to be both daring and tough in his playmaking and scoring ability.

"The twelve players selected have incredible talent, and more importantly, we think this team has excellent leadership, great versatility and balance, and very good chemistry, which are critical parts in building a great team. I believe this team is a team all Americans can and will be proud of," Jerry added.

Carmelo and Dwyane had both been on the 2004 Olympic team and, when asked, spoke briefly about their experience. Both alluded to feeling poorly prepared and not understanding the privilege it was to represent your country in the Olympics. "I've always seen greatness in the Olympics, but that was never one of my dreams," Dwyane said. "I never really expected to be on the Olympic team, especially in my first year [as an NBA player]. I didn't have a clue what I was getting into. . . . Now, we respect the game so much. We respect the team basketball that they play internationally." Thanks to the new National Team concept, this time would be different. We had the time to grow in our understanding of the international game and of the privilege of participating in Olympic competition.

Before we left the small stage to pose for photographs holding USA uniforms, Jerry was asked the inevitable "what if" question: What if we lose? His answer was perfect, "We never worry about what *might* happen, we look forward to what *will* happen." We could not allow our team progress to be stifled by "what ifs" or the pressure of outside expectations. We had to look at our mission with a feeling of excitement for what lay ahead, not a feeling of fear for what could go wrong. Anticipation. *Not* expectation.

Our National Team situation was unique because we had to face three different sets of competition in each of three summers before reaching our goal of an Olympic gold medal. Every year, we would learn a great deal more about our competition and the international game. Additionally, much could change from summer to summer in terms of the injuries and family situations of our personnel. This is another reason why Jerry's concept of the pool of players served us so well. We were able to analyze who was available and who we would face each year and then determine who could best represent us against that competition. I can remember calling Kobe Bryant, LeBron James, and Jason Kidd prior to our selection of the 2008 Olympic roster and asking for their input. All three were deferential. "Coach, you pick the team and coach us, and we'll play," Jason told me. It felt great to know that the staff and I had their confidence.

It is important to me to emphasize the fact that because our rosters varied from summer to summer, many more players deserve recognition for the rebuilding of USA Basketball than the twelve who came home from Beijing with gold medals. We had thirty-three players make a commitment. I think a lot about the contributions of those other players, guys like Tyson Chandler, Shane Battier, Kirk Hinrich, and Chauncey Billups. I do hope they realize that they were a part of bringing the gold medal back to the United States. Because they most certainly were.

TAKE THE TIME

Take the time to choose your people. In doing so, be sure that you are asking the basic but most difficult questions. Let the answers to those questions guide the selections that you make.

Remember that choosing your people is the first decision you will make as a leader. Take the time to make it a good one. Great teams start with a base of talent but consist of a mixture of experienced people who bring instant credibility and institutional understanding, and young players who bring energy and keep you fresh. But be sure that all these individuals are united by a foundation of character that will make them want to give of themselves to be a part of something bigger.

In choosing your people, remember also that you are establishing the foundation for trusting relationships. *Take the time to conduct personal interviews, face-to-face when possible.* Lay everything on the line. Be forthright about what is expected, and don't be afraid to let your people know a little about who you are and why you believe in the team cause. These initial meetings are the first indication of how your team members will communicate with one another.

Leaders sometimes get caught up too early in what the mission will be. And the mission is crucially important. But your team's people are the ones who are going to accomplish that mission. Before you get into the details of your strategy, your X's and O's, you have to decide first who is the X and who is the O.

TIME TO UNDERSTAND
CONTEXT

I believe it is the duty of individuals and teams in any profession to understand the context surrounding what they are trying to accomplish. If you work for a bank or an investing team, you need to appreciate the rise and fall of our economy over the years. Your family team should know about your heritage, where you came from, and how you got to be where you are. And since the purpose of our team was to compete for an Olympic gold medal, we certainly needed to know the history of USA Basketball in the Olympics.

I have been involved with basketball throughout my life as a player, an assistant coach, and a head coach. Through my experience, I believe I have gained a solid knowledge of the history of the game in the United States. In my involvement with USA Basketball over the years, I have also learned a fair amount about international ball.

But in taking on the responsibilities of national coach, I had to face the reality that I did not know the international game specifically as well as I knew basketball in general. My comprehension of context was not focused enough for this endeavor. So I became an avid student of the international game. I tried to learn more about the past, why we won and why we lost. I had to look at things from the international point of view, not the point of view with which I was most familiar. Before embarking on this research of context, I did not understand how different American basketball and world basketball truly were.

Remember, Team USA had lost in 2004 and we lost again in the 2006 FIBA World Championship in my first year as national coach. Often leaders reevaluate their positions only after they have suffered a defeat. I learned the lesson that you should constantly analyze and evaluate where you stand within the greater context of what you are trying to accomplish. But whether your team's mission is preceded by failure or success, you have to have a complete comprehension of your current situation before you can improve upon it. Otherwise, you have no point of comparison for that improvement—no way of telling if your team has made things better or by how much.

Once you have firmly positioned yourself within the context of your industry, you as leader must consider what, if any, contextual understanding exists among members of your team. While it is likely not necessary that all team members have the same level of historical comprehension as their leader, it is your responsibility to teach your team enough context to ensure that they all understand their place within it. This helps your team understand why you train in a particular way, lending credibility to the way you choose to prepare. It also brings seriousness to your endeavor by firmly planting your group in a history that existed before you and will continue long after you are gone. Jason Kidd did a great job of describing our staff's commitment to conveying an understanding of context. "They reminded us of what happened in the past," he said, "and what the future could hold."

Moment: The Original "Dream Team" Brings Home the Gold—August 8, 1992—Barcelona, Spain

On April 7, 1989, the International Basketball Federation (FIBA) voted to allow open competition, meaning that professional athletes would be permitted to participate in international play. Prior to this decision, our Olympic teams were comprised of only college athletes. After a disappointing loss to Russia in the semifinal game of the 1988 Seoul Olympics, USA Basketball was excited to put its best foot forward in international play by tapping into the talent and worldwide renown of the National Basketball Association (NBA). And so, the first USA Basketball team to enter Olympic competition with professional players was dubbed the Dream Team. With a roster including names like Michael Jordan, Magic Johnson, Larry Bird, Charles Barkley, and David Robinson, it was definitely a basketball dream come true.

The story of the 1992 Olympic team's road to gold is a story of historic dominance. Players from the opposing teams were excited just to occupy the same court as our team. Many of them even had their families and friends snap photographs of them playing against the legends of the NBA, knowing that this was something they would tell their children about one day. They had all watched these superstars shine in the NBA, a league that was comprised predominantly of American players.

Additionally, back in the early 1990s, the NBA was still about great teams—the Lakers-Celtics rivalry of the 1980s, the emergence of the Chicago Bulls dynasty that had won back-to-back league championships in 1991 and 1992. Coming together, these guys knew what it meant to be on a team, and they were smart enough to recognize that in joining forces to play in the Olympics, they became a part of something momentous.

It is important to recognize the fact that the '92 team had dream timing as well. Russia and Yugoslavia had recently split and the great basketball talent of that region was now divided among several teams. Hall-of-Famer and Dream Team head coach Chuck Daly pointed out afterward that had the 1990 World Championship Yugoslav team been around to compete in the Olympics, the road to gold would have been much more difficult. Would the Dream Team still have won? Yes. No one could compete with them, and they knew that. They crushed every team they played, winning their games by an average margin of 43.8 points. Needless to say, the Dream Team came home from Barcelona with gold medals around their necks.

As our 2008 Olympic team came together over three summers, people were eager to draw comparisons between us and the Dream Team. While we cannot control what people say about us, I wanted to make clear from the beginning that there was no comparison. The 1992 team will always be the first to include professional players. Not only that, it will always be special in terms of the legendary status of those players. Ten of the twelve men on that team were included on a 1996 list of the fifty greatest players in the history of the NBA. Even one of the assistant coaches, Lenny Wilkens, was on that list. Undoubtedly, the individuals on the 1992 roster were already legends and the team that they formed made history. I love the way Dwyane Wade put it when he said that the 1992 team had the best name ever in sports: the Dream Team. It was the best name and it belonged to the best team. There will never be another Dream Team.

Eager to find the appropriate moniker for our 2008 Olympic team, many members of the media began to refer to us as the Redeem Team. I can see why the name caught on. It sounded good. It was clever. I never had a problem with others choosing to refer to us as such, but we never referred to ourselves as the Redeem Team. To do so would suggest a need to return to the past, recovering what was there before. Redemption alludes to the rightful restoration of what once was. And for USA Basketball, it could no longer be about trying to recover our past success in international competition. Our place at the top was no longer rightful; we had to earn it all over again. And we had to earn it operating in an international environment that had completely changed.

So if we were not to compare ourselves to the Dream Team and we were not there to redeem their success from sixteen years prior, what could we discover about our context from their story?

What could we learn from them? One thing that we did want to replicate was the fan support they had created. They had an entire country behind them. Since then, though, that internal support for USA Basketball had faded. How could we get it back? It would be crucial for us to make certain we were worthy of that same kind of support. In part, this meant ensuring that our behavior on and off the court was guided by contextual understanding—knowing our history and feeling both humbled and inspired by our place in it.

The '92 USA Basketball experience also serves as a valuable example of how to market a team. People forget that not only do the athletes and coaches receive no payment for their participation in international basketball, but we are also required to raise the money necessary to support ourselves and cover the significant expenses accumulated along the way. There were great lessons to learn from the way the Dream Team advertised, merchandised, and gained sponsor support.

But even more than all that, we can look back on the '92 team for an understanding of the direction international basketball has taken since. As with many major businesses, basketball has gone global. And, in trying to understand the whys and hows of the globalization of basketball, one can point to 1992 as a landmark year. That year, in a post-Olympic press conference, Juan Antonio Samaranch, the then president of the International Olympic Committee (IOC), said, "The Dream Team brought the basketball competition to a new level." We had raised the bar and, in a competitive world, dominance like that of the '92 team can (and did) serve as a catalyst for the improvement of the competition.

I like to think about what a twelve-year-old Pau Gasol from Spain or a teenaged Manu Ginobili from Argentina may have been thinking when they watched the United States win that gold medal. They probably thought they were watching superheroes. They might have decided that they wanted to be superheroes, too. What we have seen in worldwide basketball since then can be seen in the landscape of the NBA as well: the rise of the international player.

In the 2007–2008 season, the NBA featured 76 international players from 31 different countries and territories.

Seven years after the Dream Team dominated in Barcelona, Manu Ginobili would be chosen, in one of the great NBA draft steals of all time, as the fifty-seventh pick overall. Three other international players were chosen in the first round of that 1999 draft. And two years after that, Pau Gasol was drafted third in a first round featuring a total of six international players chosen. In fact, an examination of the NBA draft can lend insight into the rise of international basketball stars in the NBA. In the sixteen years leading up to the 1992 Olympic Games (1977–1992), 19 international players total were selected in the first rounds of NBA drafts. In the sixteen years since (1993–2008), 82 international players have gone in the first round—a growth from an average of 1.2 players to an average of 5.1 players per year. And those numbers have increased even more since. Since 2000, an average of nearly seven international players has been selected in the first rounds, including the top overall picks in 2002, 2005, and 2006. And the players are not merely highly touted going in, they are proving themselves. In the four NBA seasons leading up to the 2008 Olympics, the MVP of the entire league has been an international player three times, with Kobe Bryant finally breaking the streak just before our Olympic summer. International players were good, no doubt. And they were not merely stars in their home countries, they were competing with American stars in the NBA and, more and more frequently, they were winning.

You improve by playing against good competition. For international players, this improvement has come through two means. First, the raising of the competitive bar by the Dream Team improved the field of international team play. International teams became more focused in their training in an attempt to live up to the new standard. And second, the influx of international players in the NBA has put each individual player in the position to improve by facing the best competition in the world on a daily basis.

As their individual players became increasingly adept at playing the NBA game, the continuity of international teams ensured that these talented players were working together in great team environments. Talented players coming together in programs that focused on continuity and growth from year to year made for a tremendous combination.

Just as in any business, recognizing new competitors on a global stage must guide the way in which you proceed. As a part of this process in the basketball world, we had to understand that these countries were not merely coming into the established world of American basketball but were contributing to a changing worldwide system. They would not fit neatly into America's game but, rather, were redefining basketball as the world's game. Since James Naismith invented the game in 1891, the United States had spent many years teaching it to the world. And the world had learned it well. Now, we had to accept the fact that *we* had something to learn from *them*. We were at a point where understanding this context, for us, meant shedding the arrogant belief that the game belonged to us and that it was ours to reclaim. We had to adapt to the new landscape or, quite simply, we would lose. It is amazing to me the way the forces of globalization have played out in basketball in such a similar fashion as they have in business.

I am grateful that I was associated with the 1992 Olympic team as one of its three assistant coaches. I learned a lot from the experience, and when I was selected by Jerry Colangelo to be the national coach, I looked back on my time as Coach Daly's assistant for guidance. I was better prepared to coach the 2008 team because I had witnessed firsthand the willingness of powerful, talented individuals to make sacrifices for the benefit of a team. I knew it was possible. I'd also learned from the Dream Team that if we did this right, we would all be bonded as brothers for life. I thought, given this incredible opportunity, I'd better not mess it up.

Moment: USA Basketball Takes Home the Bronze Medal—August 28, 2004—Athens, Greece

While the 1996 Olympic team won handily and earned gold medals in Atlanta, the 2000 team saw much better competition. In the Sydney Olympics, the basketball contests were much closer, and that team won three of its eight games by 10 points or less, including a narrow escape over Lithuania in the semifinal game, 85–83. It's become increasingly obvious that in the years following the 1992 Olympics, the gap between American talent and international teams has steadily narrowed. However, since we did win in 2000, we did not immediately recognize the need for change in our methods and training. Winning clouded our thinking.

But the 2004 Olympics in Athens made everything crystal clear. The awe factor that had surrounded the 1992 Dream Team had dissipated over the twelve years since the Dream Team annihilated the competition in Barcelona. The task the 2004 team would face was a difficult one. And when you don't have time to properly prepare, difficult tends to become impossible. You find yourself thinking about the training that all the other Olympic athletes put in. Cyclists, gymnasts, and runners train their entire lives for their Olympic moment. You can't just call up an athlete four months before Olympic competition and expect them to have the time they need to prepare. I cannot imagine how our team would have fared had we assembled for the first time in May 2008.

Additionally, as the stars of the 2004 Olympic team began their NBA careers, the league had focused its marketing efforts on the promotion of the individual athlete. Trades were increasingly frequent, and it became commonplace for even the greatest athletes to spend their careers playing for two, three, four different programs. It was no longer about teams and dynasties—now it was about individual players. This contributed to the difficulty of bringing together franchise players to form a cohesive unit. Carmelo Anthony has said of his participation on that 2004 team, "It felt like we were thrown to the wolves." And they had been. Confirming there was something structurally lacking, he continued, "We didn't know what to expect."

Lesson learned. As Jerry Colangelo put it, "You can no longer beat great teams with just a group of all-stars." The international teams were not merely ad-hoc assemblages. Players became members of programs that allowed them to work together over the course of many years. They knew each other, they had great relationships, and they had complex systems that had been put in place over the course of their considerable time together. As a result, international teams were able to play together *instinctively*. It was crucial that Jerry and USA Basketball had an understanding of this context as they put together a program that would allow us to develop instinctive play as well.

I also believe it was essential to our comprehension of context that we had four players who had been on the bronze-medal winning team in '04: Carmelo Anthony, Carlos Boozer, LeBron James, and Dwyane Wade. In some ways, these guys had more at stake than the others, and they were able to help their teammates comprehend the greater context of what we were trying to accomplish. *I think it is a mistake to automatically preclude from your team individuals who have been involved in a past failure.* In fact, failure can be an essential step on the path to success. It means you have tested your limits and likely learned a great deal. If failure does occur, a leader should use it productively. In our situation, the inclusion of these individuals was critical to gaining the level of contextual understanding that would lead to our success.

Moment: USA versus China in Olympic Pool Play— August 10, 2008—Beijing, China

A very poignant moment for me as a student of basketball was the lead-up to our first game in 2008 Olympic play. I don't think it could have been designed any better. Our first opponent was the host country, China, with an up-and-coming team highlighted by the presence of two NBA superstars and Chinese national heroes in seven-foot-six Yao Ming and seven-foot Yi Jianlian. Bear in mind that the NBA regular season matchup between Yao's Houston Rockets and Yi's Milwaukee Bucks drew a larger television viewership than the Super Bowl. When you add the 27 million American viewers who watched as we took on the host country to the vast Chinese television audience, you are looking at likely the largest television viewing audience in the history of sport. Literally hundreds of millions of people were excited to watch us play.

Our guys were excited, too. Carmelo talked about the energy in the arena that night, saying, "It was crazy. It was a great atmosphere. The fans were great. The arena was great. Everybody was energetic. We were excited. China was excited. I'm pretty sure President Bush [who was in attendance] was excited. It was great." Chris Bosh said, "It's always a special thing to come and represent your country in the Olympics. Just the pride of wearing the USA on our chest was just a thrill. The leader of our country there. It was pretty patriotic for us." And Chris Paul said, "This is bigger than a playoff game. This is two countries playing against each other. The best of the best. All the anticipation leading up to the game. This is three years coming. It gets you ready to play."

We'd played five exhibition games in a summer that had taken us from our respective homes to Las Vegas, to Macau, to Shanghai, and finally to Beijing. We were ready to find out if our preparation had been sufficient.

And China was ready for us. The ovation the USA received was terrific and surpassed only by the applause reserved for the home team. As we all stood there prior to tip-off, lined up with our teams on either end of the court, I was moved hearing our national anthem before we took the court for our first Olympic contest. Almost equally as moving, though, was listening to the Chinese national anthem. You could look at their team and see the pride on their faces. Even more, you could hear that pride as the predominantly Chinese crowd in 18,000-person-capacity Wukesong Arena stood and sang along. Listening to them sing out in unison and looking at the expressions on their faces, we saw evidence of a proud nation that had truly embraced the game of basketball as a part of their culture.

Just to put in perspective the magnitude of basketball's popularity in China, our nation's total population is around 300 million. In China, around 300 million people play basketball. For people like us who see beauty in the game, it is extremely rewarding to see it embraced the world over. Moments like these clarified for us that we did not come to China merely as representatives of ourselves and our country, but as ambassadors of a great game. It was a responsibility that we took very seriously.

Appropriately, it was China's great ambassador and hometown hero, Yao Ming, who scored the game's first basket—a three-pointer twenty seconds into the game. By the end of the first quarter, we led by only four points, but we picked up our defensive effort in the second quarter to go into halftime up by 12. After an 18–5 run in the third quarter, we never looked back.

After we came through with a 101–70 win in front of an energetic crowd and the vast worldwide television audience, Kobe Bryant made a great comment, "I've never felt an environment quite like this. I've played in many big games, but the energy tonight was different. It was amazing. Look, I had five dunks in one game. That's because of the crowd. The last time I had five dunks in a game, I think I was seventeen. And that's all because of the energy in this crowd. I think they knew that history was being made tonight. Obviously, it was a proud moment for their country. You could feel the electricity. It was a different kind of energy. I am fortunate to have played in four NBA Finals and numerous big games, but it was like you felt there was so much more support, because it was USA. Obviously you could feel how proud the fans are of their country here in China. You just understood that it was bigger than the game. It wasn't just a finals game or a seventh game, it was bigger than that."

Moment: Dinner with Former President Bush and Former Chinese President Jiang Zemin— August 11, 2008—Beijing, China

There have been many moments in my career when I have felt impossibly lucky. Of course, I have been fortunate enough to achieve many dreams on the basketball court, and I have benefited from the company of some tremendous players and coaches throughout my career. But the times that really make me ask myself "What am *I* doing here?" are times like the dinner that I attended on August 11, 2008, at the home of the Chinese president, which is amusingly referred to as "the Red House." It was an opportunity to dine and converse with a group of extraordinary people including President George H.W. Bush, his daughter Doro Bush Koch, AT&T chairman and CEO Randall Stephenson and his wife, the current Chinese foreign minister Yang Jiechi, the former Chinese president Jiang Zemin, his wife, and his grandson. Seriously, what was I doing there?

I have had the great opportunity to get to know the elder President Bush over the past few years. We hosted a leadership forum together at Texas A&M University in April 2005, and I worked with his wife, Barbara, at her literacy advocacy event the following year. So when he invited me to dinner in Beijing, I readily accepted.

For the first part of the dinner I listened as the elder President Bush described the state of affairs in the United States to the Chinese officials. You could tell that he commanded their respect and that he had taken the time to understand their culture and appreciate their values. Regardless of one's political affiliation, George H.W. Bush's relationship with the Chinese should serve as an example to anyone who wishes to operate in a global environment. He talked about the economy and even the upcoming November presidential election. Then former Chinese President Jiang talked about the state of affairs in China. It was a conversation that any interested American citizen would have been eager to hear. It was like two old friends getting up-to-date on each other's families and neighborhoods—except their neighborhoods happened to be entire countries and their families were national populations. I loved listening to that conversation. It reminded me that there are good people working for us behind the scenes in ways we do not fully understand or appreciate.

After that, the elder President Bush asked AT&T Chairman Stephenson to speak about his business and give his view on the current situation in the United States. Then, the president asked me to talk a little about my business, which was very humbling, considering that my "business" is basketball. Since we had just played against the Chinese national team, I told them how exciting it was to witness their passion for the game. I also mentioned something that I really believe to be true: how fortunate China is to have Yao Ming as a leader and cultural icon. The large Chinese delegation that marched in the Opening Ceremonies could not have had a better representative carrying their flag than Yao. How illustrative of the global growth of basketball is the fact that five countries had basketball players as their standard-bearers—and none of them were from the United States?

President Bush also asked that I give the Chinese contingent my sense of the Olympics thus far. I had three words for them: organized, clean, and friendly. The Chinese had earned much respect for the exceptional job they did as hosts.

When we sat down at a large, circular table for dinner, the conversation continued. I will always remember the moment when President Bush informed the guests that I was a graduate of West Point. My credibility increased instantly, and everyone listened intently as I described my experiences there. I told them that West Point taught me failure was not a destination; it also taught me how to test my limits and change them. Because of West Point, I understood what it means to play for the three letters on the front of the jersey and not for the name on the back.

If I hadn't realized it before, this cemented for me how crucial it was that we represent our country in the best possible manner. We needed to be respectful of our opponents, reverent of this stage, and gracious throughout.

Rare times like these make me reflect on the big, *big* picture. Certainly bringing the Olympic gold in basketball back to the United States is a worthy and honorable goal. But being a guest at this meal served as a reminder that this Olympics was an historical one on a global stage, not merely on the basketball hardwood. This moment, the incredible Opening Ceremonies, and numerous other moments during our time in Beijing reminded me of one of the primary things the 2008 Beijing Olympics were about: an opportunity for a country to prove itself a contender among world powers and to put its progress on display. And what an impressive display China put on.

TAKE THE TIME

Take the time to understand context. While certainly the history of USA Basketball, the globalization of the game, and the emergence of China as a world power were not topics of discussion in our team huddles or the halftime locker room, they provided the mental and motivational backdrop for our team's purpose. By learning how we got where we were, we also learned how to get where we wanted to be. And as the old saying reminds us, those who do not learn from the past are doomed to repeat it. Fortunately for us, we had a terrific understanding of our past—particularly our recent past—and we decided that we would not repeat it. By placing your team within its greater context, you can identify those lessons from the past that will guide you in your preparation and training.

In learning about the context of your team, you as the leader can gain an appreciation of where you fall within the larger framework of global affairs. Accomplishing this brings a seriousness to your undertaking. It gives you and your team the chance to realize the significance of your goals. When you are on the court, on the playing field, or in the boardroom, your team should feel as if your undertaking is of the utmost importance. That's the way you should play.

TIME TO GAIN
PERSPECTIVE

No matter how important you believe yourself to be, there is always something bigger than you. As your team pursues its goal, it is vital that you maintain a sense of perspective. And I believe that context and perspective are very different. While context gives you a sense of where your endeavor falls within the larger picture of your industry, perspective should provide a feeling of humility in the pursuit of your goal. Where context brings seriousness and focus, perspective keeps you humble.

Proper perspective also adds depth to your mission. It moves you beyond the superficial and taps into the emotion we all want to feel. I subscribe to one of the most basic methods of teaching: hearing, seeing, and doing. The hearing and seeing are easy. Even the doing is easy on a logistical level—that is what practice is all about. But to get to this deeper level, to have this perspective I'm referring to, you have to give your team opportunities to *feel*, to experience the emotion that can accompany a team endeavor. Imagine how much better your team can become if you can engage the mind and spirit of each individual and, even more, imagine the level your team can achieve if you share the *same* mind and spirit.

With a team, you have the potential to accomplish things that you could never do on your own. As such, every group ought to understand and internalize that it is a privilege to be on a team. For USA Basketball, we needed to recognize that it was an even greater privilege to be on a team that had the opportunity to represent our country. In our effort to reinforce that perspective, we tried to constantly put our team in positions where we all could really *feel*.

Moment: Colonel Bob Brown and Three Wounded Warriors Address the Team—July 22, 2006— Las Vegas, Nevada

The first summer that our team came together to practice and participate in the FIBA World Championship, I immediately wanted to find out if they had the capacity to feel at a deeper level, to see if they were capable of the perspective that I knew we needed. At one of our early meetings, I invited some guests to address our team. Colonel Bob Brown (now a general), a player whom I coached at West Point, came to Las Vegas and brought three wounded soldiers along with him: Captain D.J. Skelton, Sergeant Christian Steele, and Captain Scott Smiley. Colonel Brown spoke first, writing two words on the whiteboard in the meeting room: *selfless service*. "What makes teams great is selfless service," he said. "It's putting the needs of someone else before yourself. On the basketball court that may be diving for a loose ball or taking a charge. On the battlefield it may be running into a wall of bullets or putting your life on the line for someone."

The three wounded soldiers that Colonel Brown introduced to us had all put the needs of their fellow soldiers before their own. Captain D.J. Skelton was wounded in Iraq when a rocket-propelled grenade (RPG) struck him and took his left eye. But he did not let this dishearten him. Instead, he allowed it to inspire him to act for change in the way the Army dealt with its wounded warriors, helping to draft legislation that would give insurance to wounded soldiers and writing a handbook to assist others in their recoveries. Despite his injury, after Captain Skelton left our training camp he headed to Ranger School, where he would take command of a group of young soldiers.

Like Captain Skelton, Sergeant Steele continued his Army career even after being wounded, losing a finger, and suffering severe shrapnel wounds to his neck, back, and legs as the result of a suicide attack in a military dining facility in Iraq, an incident in which twenty-two of his fellow soldiers were killed.

After hearing from Captain Skelton and Sergeant Steele, Colonel Brown introduced Captain Scott Smiley and told the team about the young captain's bravery. As a suicide car bore down on the Stryker armored combat vehicle carrying him and his men, Captain Smiley stayed up with his head and body exposed and continued firing at the oncoming vehicle, causing it to explode before it could take out his Stryker. In doing so, he was hit by a piece of shrapnel in his eyes, blinding him permanently. But his bravery had saved the lives of his teammates.

Colonel Brown explained to us that, despite his disability, Scott Smiley also fought to stay in the Army. "I was over fighting in Iraq," he told us, "and I got a call saying that Scottie Smiley wants to stay in the Army, and I didn't know what to do. I've never had a guy who was blind try to stay in. But he fought to stay." As he spoke about Scott's courage, Colonel Brown was overcome with emotion and, after pausing for a moment to collect himself, he said, "So, he's in. And he's still serving. And, as Scott told me earlier, he's no different than before. He had problems then and he just has different problems now. That's a hero."

In continuing his emotional presentation to our team, Colonel Brown told us three things about selfless service: it's about being a part of a cause greater than yourself, it's what makes great teams and leaders, and it's tough. If these three young men could do the heroic things that they did and continue to selflessly serve at the highest of levels, we could certainly play good defense, we could dive on the court for a loose ball, and we could surely represent USA Basketball in a manner that would make our country proud. In gaining this perspective, we had to realize that our selfless service as basketball players would never be at the heroic level of theirs as soldiers, but we could allow them to be our teachers.

Before he left, Colonel Brown distributed flags to each one of our players, flags that had been worn on the uniforms of soldiers serving overseas. He asked that we wear them on our warm-ups and said to us, "When you look at that flag on your uniform, you'll know you're playing much more than a basketball game; you're playing for your country."

Our guests were invited to attend our team's practice later that day. The USA Basketball staff arranged for Captain Smiley to wear a set of earphones connected to lavalier microphones worn by Dwyane Wade and Gilbert Arenas. The two of them did the play-by-play for Scott throughout the workout. This way, he could experience our practice even though he couldn't see it. One of my favorite moments was when Dwyane Wade, seated on one of the sideline benches for a rest, said into his microphone, "Scottie, can you hear me?" Scottie nodded from his seat across the court. "When we put these jerseys on we feel a lot of pride, walking around with USA on our chests. I know you all have a lot of pride. You guys are role models for a lot of us out here. We don't get a chance to tell you but you all are role models for us and we respect what you do for our country."

Dwyane got it. He had perspective. He understood that people like Scott Smiley are the real heroes and that we could emulate them by representing our country based on an understanding of selfless service. He realized that while NBA superstars are role models for so many youngsters, we as adults look up to people like Scott Smiley, D.J. Skelton, Christian Steele, and Bob Brown.

Our sense of perspective showed us that the military's stakes are much greater than those we would ever face on the court. There is clearly no comparison between taking a charge in a basketball game and putting your life on the line in a combat situation. But what I hoped our team could tap into is that we do have something in common with the soldiers—who we represent. In listening to true American heroes talk about selfless service, we could gain a better understanding of what it means to be an American.

In that moment when Colonel Brown and the wounded warriors

spoke, I gained a better sense of who we were. Scanning the faces of our team, I first noticed Coach D'Antoni wiping tears from his eyes. The normally boisterous LeBron James was moved to a serious and respectful silence. And I wondered if Chris Paul was paying attention when I noticed his head facing downward. But when he looked up, he was crying, too. It was a great feeling to learn that my team could access a depth of emotion that would bond us even more closely in our endeavor. Now I knew that my team had heart.

Moment: Visit and Practice at US Military Bases in South Korea—August 14 and 16, 2006—Camp Yongsan and Camp Casey, South Korea

Before heading to Japan to play in the 2006 World Championships, our team traveled to two Army posts in South Korea to visit our American troops stationed there. One of my favorite moments from those visits was when our team and staff were each given a set of fatigues, known as ACUs (Army Combat Uniform), with our names on them. Our guys were like kids putting them on. So often, people wear the jerseys of Carmelo Anthony or Dwight Howard or Chris Paul. Those players are heroes to a lot of people. But on this day, we were able to wear the uniforms of *our* heroes, letting them know that we both honored and thanked them.

Another tribute to the soldiers that developed on that trip was our players' saluting after making good plays. Instead of a chest bump or a high five, they started to salute each other and the crowd as a sign of respect for our military. This continued through the rest of our summer together.

We had traveled overseas and were on our way to Japan to compete in the World Championships. We would be away from our homes and families for forty-five days. But, visiting the Army posts in South Korea put in perspective for us what it *really* means to serve our country overseas. These soldiers leave their families for months and even years at a time. They truly are America's team. We simply wanted to learn enough from them so that we could become America's basketball team.

Moment: Returning the Favor—June 25, 2008— Fort Leavenworth, Kansas

Two summers after he had brought the three wounded warriors to speak to my team at our training camp in Las Vegas, General Bob Brown invited me to speak to some members of his team at Fort Leavenworth, Kansas. There, the leadership of five Army brigades held a weeklong meeting in preparation for each brigade's upcoming deployment to Iraq. Now the deputy commander of the Twenty-fifth Infantry Division, General Brown thought that I could provide some insights on teamwork and leadership as they embarked on their missions overseas. After the incredible impact he had on the formation of our team, I was excited to have the opportunity to return the favor.

When introducing me, General Brown talked about the importance of "love of country" and how it should serve as the foundation of all we do. He described his 2006 visit with our team and how, since then, Scott Smiley had been named Army Soldier of the Year and had decided to take two years to further his education at Duke's Fuqua School of Business before continuing his military career. After he showed a video of his talk to our team in 2006, General Brown gave me the opportunity to speak.

There is a certain feeling of inadequacy when you address a group of soldiers. Though I had done a lot of public speaking, I had never experienced the level of discomfort that I did in preparing to speak to a room that contained five generals and their men and women. I said, first and foremost, what a true honor it was for me to be there. But what else could I possibly say to this group? I just decided to speak from the heart. "I don't know what I'm doing up here speaking to you guys," I said. "We just play basketball. You protect our right to do that."

Because they and their teams were about to embark on extremely important missions, I felt I would try to give them some thoughts on team building. I talked about how ego can be a good thing, but you have to come together to form a team ego that is greater than each player's individual ego. I talked about two being better than one only if two can act as one. And I talked about building a trust among team members that would create the ability to react at a moment's notice with no questions asked. I honestly believe that they enjoyed my talk, and I hope it was helpful.

What happened that afternoon was mutual motivation. Talking to those men and women about serving the United States helped give meaning to our endeavor, and it gave me a terrific feeling of patriotism as I headed to Las Vegas for our Olympic team mini-camp. We share with our soldiers a love of country and a commitment to represent the United States with extreme pride. Whatever I was able to give them in the form of inspiration, that was an honor for me. Whatever connection they felt with our Olympic team as we pursued the gold in Beijing, that was an honor for all of us. But we cannot repay them for the service that they do for our entire nation, a service that often goes thankless. We are all patriotic, but our soldiers are the true patriots. We could only hope to make General Brown and the rest of them proud as we embarked on our respective missions. We all wanted to come home winners.

Moment: Team Promotional Trip—June 30, 2008—New York, New York

Originally, I looked at the packed itinerary for our Olympic team's short trip to New York and thought of it as a necessary publicity blitz in our effort to earn public support. It ended up being one of those moments whose importance I would not fully understand until later. It was a short, but action-packed, twenty-four hours.

We were set to take off for New York on a noon charter out of Las Vegas, where we had just finished mini-camp. However, there was a weather delay, and we ended up waiting on the runway for three hours before finally taking off. When we reached New York airspace, weather on the ground prevented us from landing for an additional hour. I joked later with the team that Jerry Colangelo, ever attentive to detail, had planned this nine-hour flight in order to prepare us for the long trip to Beijing.

Despite the fact that it was midnight and we were all exhausted, we followed our original plan to visit the USA Basketball museum that Nike had established in Harlem honoring the history of USA Basketball. The first thing we saw when we walked through the doors was a dramatically spotlighted glass case in which hung the jerseys of all twelve members of our Olympic roster. The walls to either side of the case were covered, floor to ceiling, with images of our players and of Olympic teams of the past. It was a remarkable exhibit—and it had a powerful impact on our players and staff.

We didn't get into our rooms at the Plaza Hotel until after 2:00 a.m. Most of the guys, myself included, had to get up at 5:00 a.m. to make the rounds of the morning television shows. Not one of our players complained, they were all on time, and they all represented our team in the best way possible. I was really proud of the way they handled themselves.

After our morning, in which we fulfilled various individual media obligations, we reconvened as a team on a large, three-deck tour boat at a pier on the Lower East Side of Manhattan. At 9:00 a.m. we sailed out to Ellis Island for a team photo in front of the Statue of Liberty. For many of us, that boat ride was a profound and emotional time. "It brings it all into focus," Jerry said. "It firms everything up about how passionate we are about our goal."

It was incredible to think that only two generations ago, my ancestors crossed an ocean with what must have been an overwhelming sense of both fear and hope. I think about the courage of those people. For them, the hope outweighed the fear and they headed to America, counting on the promise of opportunity. Reflecting on what the Statue of Liberty symbolizes, Kobe Bryant noted that it was the first thing that immigrants saw when they arrived in America. Kobe put the sentiment beautifully when he said, "This is where a lot of dreams started."

It put in perspective what our ancestors did a hundred years ago, what their courage had done for us. I imagined my grandfather Josef Pituch arriving at Ellis Island in 1906 after a nearly three-week journey across an ocean. One generation later, Josef's daughter Emily married William Krzyzewski, who found it necessary to change his name to William Kross in order to avoid ethnic discrimination. Only one generation after that, William and Emily's son would coach a United States team in the Olympics. I wondered what Josef would have thought of that. It was a powerful moment. And a humbling one.

Moment: Meeting US Standard-Bearer Lopez Lomong— August 7, 2008—Beijing, China

As noted, Yao Ming carried China's flag in the 2008 Olympic Opening Ceremonies. Germany's was carried by Dirk Nowitzki. Manu Ginobili was Argentina's standard-bearer. These were all colleagues of the players on our team, fellow NBA stars whom they knew well. But an NBA star would not carry the American flag, though the US contingent had plenty from which to choose. Our standard-bearer was someone our players likely would have never known. And there could not have been a better choice.

The day before the Olympic Games were set to begin, United States Olympic Committee (USOC) Chairman Peter Ueberroth brought the US standard-bearer to meet our team. You could see that Lopez Lomong was excited to meet our players. I had read about Lopez and knew his incredible story, so I asked him to tell our team about his life. I wanted them to understand exactly who the athletes had elected to carry our flag.

A humble young man, Lopez originally told our team just the basics: he was from the Sudan and had proudly become an American citizen in 2007. After some prodding from me, he reluctantly told our team more about his life. Lopez was one of Sudan's "Lost Boys," one of the more than 26,000 children who were displaced by the civil war in that region. Abducted from church when he was six, Lopez escaped and sought refuge at a camp near Nairobi, where he remained for ten years. Believing him to be dead, Lopez's parents even had a funeral for him and mourned his passing. As the result of an essay he wrote about the goals he would set for himself if given the opportunity to move to America, Lopez became one of thousands of Lost Boys relocated to the United States through charities and placed with foster families. At the age of sixteen, Lopez was taken in by the Rogers family of upstate New York. Since then, some amazing things had happened for him: he had been reunited with his birth mother, returned for the first time to his native village, won two Division-I NCAA national championships in the indoor 3,000-meter and outdoor 1,500-meter, and became a naturalized citizen of the United States. Now he was going to carry the American flag at the Opening Ceremonies of the Olympic Games. What an incredible story.

When he finished speaking I said to him, "Lopez, I want to thank you for our entire team and tell you that there is no one else that we would rather have carry our flag." I could tell by the looks on our players' faces the impact that Lopez's story had on them, and I loved watching as they each embraced him or shook his hand.

In an interview following the Olympics, Chairman Ueberroth was asked about his most memorable moment from the Olympic games. He responded with the story of Lopez meeting our basketball team. "We go and there are all these big guys slouched in their chairs, arms going everywhere. Coach Krzyzewski had researched and read the story of this guy. He said, 'Tell them your story. Tell them about so and so. Tell them about this.' The players went from slouching in chairs to standing, and from standing to standing politely and from hats on to hats off. Each player all of the sudden wanted to hug him. We all have tough backgrounds, but this young man's story was incredible."

As you give your team more and more opportunities to *feel*, those emotions come more easily. I knew since that meeting with the wounded warriors back in 2006 that my team had heart, and now it was becoming increasingly clear that we had *one* heart.

TAKE THE TIME

Take the time to gain perspective. Let that perspective operate along with your understanding of context. Context should serve as your guide in what you do on the court, or on the playing field, or in the boardroom. It brings about the feeling that what you are doing is of great consequence. And believing in the significance of what you are doing while you are doing it is good—in fact, it's the only way to compete. When we were out on that court, I wanted our players to feel like winning the gold medal was the most important thing in the world.

But when you step off that basketball court or outside of that boardroom, you have to realize that it's really not. There are things that are bigger than you. This sense of perspective should guide your team's behavior and the way in which you relate to those around you. Your team should appreciate the fact that your actions and words off the court are still a reflection on the entire team, on your brand. Ego and humility are not mutually exclusive. You can have both. You *should* have both.

Perspective also allows you and your team to access an intensity of emotion that you could not feel otherwise. By exposing our team to people like Bob Brown, Scott Smiley, and Lopez Lomong, by taking them to places like military posts and the Statue of Liberty, they had the opportunity to feel and experience things in life that are much more profound than basketball.

To be a world-class champion, you have to have both context and perspective. You have to understand how big and how small you are, and be able to internalize both. When you have that combination, you can approach your undertaking at a new level, one that allows your emotions to bring out your best. Your team will know that together you have to produce a performance worthy of that stage. In our particular situation, we understood what the Olympics were, we understood where basketball was, and we had that feeling of perspective in representing our country. We were in the Olympic moment. Context defines your moment, and perspective allows you to make the most of it.

TIME TO FORM RELATIONSHIPS

The single most important factor in bringing a team together is the formation of relationships. But in order to engage in a discussion of how great relationships are formed on a team, we must first define what a great relationship entails. What makes one relationship more lasting, more meaningful, and more successful than another?

The relationships that a leader wants to see develop among his or her team are based on communication. In pressure situations, members of a team will often revert to individual instincts, and individual instincts are often synonymous with selfish instincts. Talk—both on the court and off—allows your team to think collectively, and when that happens you come to rely on group instincts. Chris Bosh said during the experience, "Talk is contagious." In building relationships with your team, you definitely want communication to spread. On my basketball teams, I try to instill three systems. Our offensive and defensive systems comprise those X and O strategies that we implement on the court. But most important of all is our system of communication. In another business, you may have more than three systems, you may have fewer. But I believe that every successful team has one system in common and that is communication.

I emphasize honesty in forming strong systems of communication. That is why in choosing your people it is important to be up front and honest with them right from the start. Communication brings about trust. One facilitates the other. Eventually two people who communicate and trust one another develop the ability to act as one. In a trusting relationship, you attempt to have no surprises. When you talk, you look one another in the eye and you tell the truth. There is no time wasted trying to figure out what your teammate is hiding or what his or her ulterior motives may be. When you are in the heat of competition, time is precious, and you need to be able to operate at a moment's notice.

In addition to communication and trust, respect is a fundamental building block for strong relationships. Jerry Colangelo says it best: "You don't demand respect, you earn it." Of course, this takes time. In asking for that three-year commitment from each player and staff member, Jerry gave us the time we needed to earn one another's respect.

As communication, trust, and respect improve over time, your team grows stronger. Team members begin to learn that coming together is not just a sacrifice—but that it has its rewards. While you may be giving up some individual ego in favor of a collective one, you get much more than you give. What you get is the chance to be around people who can make you better every day. You can become each other's teachers. *In a team environment, the talent and expertise of the person next to you is not a threat, but an opportunity.*

When a team first begins to form, there is always a learning curve. Your group dynamic, your efficiency, and your effectiveness will improve greatly from your team's beginning to its end. But that being said, it is also natural for things to be shaky at first. The learning curve has to do primarily with being in unchartered waters. Sufficient time must be spent getting to know one another and building a foundation. In basketball, this may mean focusing only on X's and O's too much early on. In another business, it may mean getting too far into your strategic plan before you are connected as a team. In my experience, you have to really know someone in order to bring out the best in them. In a new group, allowing time for personal connections to develop is essential. As a leader, you should always try to put your team in a position to build this foundation.

People often talk about bonding. So much so, in fact, that "bonding" has become a word that some people use sarcastically. But no matter how clichéd it may sound, a team has to bond. And bonding does not just happen on its own. Time must be dedicated to the process. Conscious effort must be made. And remember that relationships cannot be cemented solely in your team's meetings or at practices. There have to be other chances to connect. You may have an individual on your team who never says a word in a meeting but will open up over a shared meal. Memories of what you accomplished in the boardroom should be interspersed with memories from a group get-together or retreat. Once your people really know each other, you will see that reflected in the way they do business.

Give your team members these chances to interact off the court or outside of the boardroom in a less serious environment that allows room for one of the greatest relationship builders of all: humor. There is absolutely a place for humor in the formation of teams, basketball, business, or otherwise. Looking back, I think a lot of our USA Basketball players were surprised to find that I even had a sense of humor. In truth, humor is a huge part of how I have related to all my teams. Humor is also an effective tool in combating short attention spans. When you are speaking to your team and recognize their attention span is growing short, a well-placed injection of levity can reel your team back in. I often try to strategically time my jokes in order to regain the focus of my team. Then, I can follow that moment of humor with a strong point that I want to get across.

Moment: First Gathering of the Coaching Staff—
May 6, 2006—Phoenix, Arizona

One of the things that benefited me most from the experience with the National Team was being around my talented staff: Syracuse University Coach Jim Boeheim, New York Knicks Coach Mike D'Antoni, and Portland Trail Blazers Coach Nate McMillan. Being in the trenches with some of the best minds in the game allowed us all to improve individually, and I do believe we returned to Duke, Syracuse, New York, and Portland better coaches than we were when we started our three years together. A huge moment for our relationship was when we all gathered as a group for the very first time. It was the night that Coach D'Antoni, who was the Phoenix Suns coach at that time, had defeated the Los Angeles Lakers in Game Seven of their first-round NBA Playoffs series to advance to the Western Conference Semifinals. I had attended the game with Jerry Colangelo and Sean Ford. Sean works full-time with USA Basketball under the title of assistant executive director for USAB's Men's Programs. But really I think his title should be "the main man." There was only one person who made it through the entire Olympic experience without a single turnover. That guy was Sean Ford.

You have to flip all the way to page 113 of the 116-page 2008 USA Basketball Men's Olympic Team Media Guide to find Sean's name. Even then, it is in fine print on the bottom right-hand corner of the page. Nowhere in it is he pictured. But Sean was as essential to the success of our team as anyone. He was the man with the greatest institutional memory. He took care of what people often call the little things. People call them that, but these details require *big*-time commitment, organization, and planning. In team building, the person in charge of these things must be an individual you can trust without question and whose attention to detail is unsurpassed. These are the people who work the hardest of all, specializing in meticulousness and allowing the leaders to lead and the players to play.

If you as the leader never have to worry about the things that can beat you internally, imagine how focused you can be on your external competition. Because of Sean, the players and coaches never had any distractions. The more I think about it, the more amazed I am that we did not encounter a single problem with our schedule and organization. It makes me wonder how many problems Sean solved before they ever came to my or Jerry's attention. In building your team, remember the fundamental importance of people like Sean and the need for the relationship the leader forms with this individual to be one of the strongest and most trusting of all.

So, on that Saturday in 2006, Sean, Jerry Colangelo, and I went directly from the Suns game to an Italian restaurant in Phoenix called Bianco's, where we would be joined by Coach D'Antoni and the rest of the staff. The restaurant staff seated us at a long, outdoor picnic table, and the setting created a warm environment. It was really a special moment: all of us arriving from our separate locations, from our real lives, and joining together for the first time as a USA Basketball staff. The next morning we would get down to business and strategy but that night was about coming together as a family for the first time. It was about just being people, about having a relationship that went beyond the workplace.

There was definitely eager anticipation around that table, but there was also an unknown. We knew we were taking the first step on a long journey together, but we still knew so little about each other or about how we would reach our destination. Two and a half years later, at the celebration following our gold-medal victory, Sean Ford said to me, "I really wish I had a photograph of that first meal we shared as a staff. If I had that photo, I'd put it in a frame right next to the photo of all of us on the court tonight. Here we are where we hoped we'd be back then, but back then we had no idea how we'd get here." I thought that was amazing. But what amazed me even more was to think how much our relationships had grown and developed since then, and how ev-

eryone who sat at that Bianco's dinner table that night would be
bonded for life.

Moment: Establishing Our Pre-Practice Meeting— July 19, 2006—Las Vegas, Nevada

During those first two summers we spent as a team, we learned
about each other while simultaneously learning about the international game. LeBron James expressed it perfectly when he said,
"You have to be a family first to be a team." And being a family
begins and ends with communication.

The staff and players all arrived at our first training camp in
mid-July 2006. As we settled into what our team's customs would
be, I wanted to immediately establish a set pattern of communication. For the next three summers, we would gather in a hotel
meeting room prior to every single practice. We had those rooms
set up like classrooms, with our players at tables facing forward,
facilitating an attentive environment. We wanted the atmosphere
to convey an understanding that this would be fun, but that there
was also business to be done.

Sometimes these meetings would be only five minutes long,
but we maintained them as a consistent routine throughout our
time together. These meetings were an integral part of instilling
our system of communication. Had we all merely assembled on
the team bus and driven immediately to practice, we would start
out disjointed, with everybody on a different page. But by having
that meeting, when we arrived at the gym, we were one. Without
meeting beforehand, I would not see my guys' faces until practice
began. You cannot build or sustain a relationship that way. The
importance of face-to-face communication is a very simple concept, but those opportunities are becoming more scarce in our
fast-paced and increasingly technological society.

In the end, we found that daily meeting to be even more important in forming relationships than we had originally anticipated.

Because we did it every day, because those meetings connected us before we even boarded the bus, it meant that every day we had the potential to have a great practice. Looking back, it was perhaps the most fundamental moment in facilitating our team's system of communication.

Moment: Dwyane Wade Arrives to Support His Teammates—September 1, 2007—Las Vegas, Nevada

Despite the fact that knee and shoulder surgeries prevented Dwyane Wade from playing in 2007, he did not want to miss out on the essential team building that took place over that summer. He recognized that the makeup of Team USA had changed—we had been joined by Kobe and Jason—and he wanted to establish himself as a member of this team, too. Dwyane had come for our inter-squad scrimmage in late July and arrived in time to support us in the semifinals and final game of the FIBA Americas Championship. He sat with us on the bench for each game, dressed in slacks and a USA Basketball polo, just like our coaching staff.

Dwyane showed his commitment when he came to Vegas that summer and I felt my connection with him continue to grow. Unfortunately, over the 2007–2008 Miami Heat season, Dwyane struggled with his injury. He was not even able to play in the Heat's last two months, and speculation grew that Dwyane would never be the All-Star caliber player he once was. Regardless, he had shown a real commitment to our team, and I wanted to show a commitment to him. I called him a number of times during his recovery. In each conversation, he always emphasized his desire to come back and play in the Olympics. Many raised questions about whether or not he should. But Miami Heat President Pat Riley and the entire organization were completely supportive.

I remember one phone call in particular that I had with Dwyane. I was at the beach with my family in May 2008, spending some time together before the upcoming hectic summer. My phone rang and I saw on the caller ID that it was Dwyane. My family joked in the background about whether or not I was in his "Fave 5" and I conveyed their message to Dwyane. He laughed as I stepped out on the porch to continue our conversation in private.

"So," I said to him, "will you be ready?"

"I'll be ready," he replied.

I got very serious with him, "Dwyane," I said, "I want you to know that I believe in you." Often leaders take for granted that gifted people like these NBA players automatically have the confidence that they need to perform at the highest level. Dwyane Wade had been MVP of the 2006 NBA Playoffs Finals. He was a champion. But even champions need someone to believe in them. I wanted him to know that I was that person.

Because I didn't know where Dwyane would be offensively coming back from his injury, I thought he should come into our Olympic summer with a defensive mind-set. I continued, "I'm going to need you to play defense. I mean, when we play Argentina and Kobe is out of the game, who will guard Manu Ginobili?"

"I will," he replied.

"Exactly," I said to him. "That's how I see it too. You are going to be extremely important to this team. And I believe you will be ready." When we finished our conversation, I was excited that Dwyane and I were on the same page. And I did feel like he would bring a lot to our team. But Dwyane brought more to our endeavor than anyone on our staff ever expected—defensively, offensively, and as a leader on the court. As our top scorer, he may arguably have been the MVP of our National Team's Olympic summer. Dwyane's journey back began when he showed up to support his teammates and proved his commitment to all of us.

Moment: Camp Wynn—September 2, 2007—
Las Vegas, Nevada

The summer of 2007 culminated with our team's victory over Argentina in the FIBA Americas Championship final. A terrific twelve-man roster plus Dwyane Wade supporting them from the bench won a tournament together for the first time, earning our right to participate in the 2008 Beijing Olympics. Winning gave us all a great feeling, but it also meant it was time to say good-bye until we met again the next summer. We felt like kids leaving summer camp and knowing we would not see our friends again until next year, friends we would miss.

That night, our great friends Steve and Elaine Wynn, owners of the Wynn Las Vegas resort where we had all stayed, held a wonderful celebration for our team. Appropriately, the celebration was called "Camp Wynn." The room was decorated like an end-of-summer camp party: red and white checkered linens on picnic tables with banners and flags everywhere. Hot dogs, barbecue, hamburgers, and french fries were served in addition to some of the Wynn's finest gourmet offerings. All our players, staff, their families and friends were invited to share a meal and celebrate our accomplishment. It was an opportunity to bring our extended families together to become a part of the family we had formed as a team.

But even though that summer was drawing to a close, the Wynns were careful not to treat the party as the end of something. Indeed, it was far from the end for our team. Somehow, they made it feel like a beginning, even distributing T-shirts saying, "What happens in Vegas, repeats in Beijing"—reminding us that we would be back together the next summer for our ultimate test. They helped us make certain that the feeling we had that night would carry over into the way we began the following summer. Not only that, the extended families and friends were included in that feeling. Down to the man, all the players on our rosters over the three summers are good guys. So, it was not a difficult decision to include their families and friends in what we were trying to accomplish. All were invited, and many came. I remember Deron Williams introducing me to his wife and two young daughters. I remember spending time with LeBron's mother, Gloria. And my wife had a great conversation with Kobe's wife, Vanessa. They didn't just watch their sons, brothers, husbands, and friends play, they were a part of it. We became a bigger, stronger family that night—one ready to pursue the gold in 2008.

When we reconvened the following summer to pursue our Olympic dream, I knew that we had been successful in forming relationships because there was a wonderful feeling of reunion.

The "Camp Wynn" party was just one of the numerous examples of the support USA Basketball received from the Wynns. It was a tremendous partnership. Throughout the course of our team's time together, Steve and Elaine helped set a tone, creating an atmosphere conducive to excellence, from the way their hotel hosted and cared for our team in each of our three summers to the way that they personally cheered for our guys at the games. The attention to detail and incredible support they and their staff provided helped us establish the foundation for what we had to accomplish. I will never forget the video that they arranged to have playing in each of our hotel rooms the night after our exhibition game against the Canadian National Team in 2008, prior to leaving for the Olympics. On it, Steve and Elaine both bid us good luck, and then members of the Wynn Las Vegas staff that had tended to all our needs for three years came on-screen, one by one, with their best wishes for our endeavor.

Locations, atmospheres, and environments can set a tone. But the relationships you form set a tone as well. Being associated with the Wynns personally has made me better, and their relationship with our team helped us immensely in accomplishing our goal. What relationships can you form to help set a tone for your team? How can that outside support serve to strengthen you internally?

Moment: Team Dinner at Morton's Steakhouse— July 29, 2008—Macau, China

With the exception of our training meals on game days, our National Team did not typically eat dinner as a group. Because the players were giving up their summers to play basketball, we tried to give the guys the opportunity to eat on their own and to take advantage of their free time. Particularly in Macau and Shanghai, we wanted them to enjoy their personal time before getting down to business in Beijing. But, in the interest of always keeping my team informed, I would consistently tell our players of the coaches' plan for the evening. We had agreed that there would be no surprises and I wanted the players to know that we were always available to them.

On our first night in Macau, I told the team that the coaching staff and I were going to dinner over at the Wynn Macau hotel. "If you want to freaking come, come," I said jokingly. "But if you don't want to freaking come, you don't have to freaking come." The guys laughed and we ended the meeting.

The next night, I said something similar to them, "Tonight, the staff is eating at Morton's. If you want to freaking come, come. But—"

LeBron interrupted, "We know, Coach, if we don't want to freaking come we don't have to freaking come." The guys laughed again and surprised us all by saying that they did want to join us for dinner. With all of us at Morton's that night, it felt like a college team on a road trip. I remember looking around the room and thinking how unbelievable it was that those guys were there. They weren't required to be there, they chose to be. You could feel that something special was happening with our team and that the bonds between us were growing stronger all the time.

Moment: Our Arrival in Beijing—August 6, 2008— Runway, Beijing Airport

Jerry and I sat together on our team's two-hour flight from Shanghai to Beijing. As we landed, we looked at one another and nodded. Words were not necessary. We were finally here. This shared look served as a reminder of everything we had worked for and everything that was at stake. Now it was time to see if our plan would work.

Putting your legacy on the line means facing the possibility of adding some "Yeah buts" to the story of your career. Someone may say, "Jerry Colangelo's Arizona Diamondbacks won a World Series." And someone could come back with, "Yeah, but his USA team couldn't get the gold medal." Another person may remark, "Coach K won three national championships." And someone could negate that by saying, "Yeah, but he couldn't take his coaching to the next level in the Olympics." Jerry and I were putting our legacies on the line, but we were doing it together. The fact that he and I both went all in united us in an uncommon way. Even when the life span of your team comes to an end, you have a lasting reward in the form of these friendships that never end.

Moment: The Intercontinental Meal Room— August 7–24, 2008—Beijing, China

Similar to the way the Camp Wynn party brought our players, coaches, and their families together at the end of our 2007 summer in Las Vegas, the group meal room at our hotel in Beijing, the Intercontinental, served to unite us all once we had crossed overseas. In one huge room, we shared three meals a day together. My family would always sit in the far, back corner because, with eight loud adults and five grandchildren under eight years old, the Polish Griswalds had a way of dominating a room. But it was great having them all there, and we found that other children would gravitate to our corner. Jim Boeheim's three young children and Mike D'Antoni's son, Michael, had a blast with my grandchildren, and Jim's grown daughter, Lizzie, got along great with my daughters. Lisa Leslie, a four-time gold-medal winner for USA Women's Basketball, had her daughter, Lauren, with her and she would come over to play, too. My youngest grandchild, Quin, even developed a crush on Kobe Bryant's youngest daughter, Gigi. At two years old, he would unabashedly hold out his arms to be picked up by Kobe, but immediately turned shy and blushed in Gigi's presence.

And it was not just the youngsters who had the opportunity to bond. The coaches and members of the team all had a chance to get to know each others' families. When LeBron came into the meal room the first morning my family was there, he immediately walked over to them, hugged my wife and each of my three daughters, shook hands with my three sons-in-law, and acknowledged all five of my grandchildren. I had the opportunity to talk to my players' mothers, to get to know their wives, and to watch them play with their children. It brought us a new level of familiarity. In that meal room, there was a sense of normalcy. It was a place where we could decompress. It really felt like one enormous family.

I have always used the words "team" and "family" interchangeably. My family is a team and my team is a family. When you can incorporate the two together—your team and your family—you create an opportunity for the relationships between everyone to grow even stronger.

Moment: LeBron Saves the Coaching Staff— August 8, 2008—Beijing, China

As team relationships grow over time and are built on that foundation of communication, trust, and respect, you can find that something else grows: caring. The Olympic Opening Ceremonies were a remarkable, once-in-a-lifetime experience. The Chinese put on an awe-inspiring show. And there is nothing quite like walking out on a track in front of ninety thousand people, as the world watches on television, and saying, "Here we are. We're America." Our team loved having the opportunity to be out on the infield of the Chinese National Stadium, or "Bird's Nest," and visit with other Olympic athletes while the rest of the countries marched into the stadium. It was a moment that really captured the spirit of the Olympic Games.

But while it was an experience I would never trade, it was also somewhat trying. We were on our feet for over six hours in the overwhelming summer heat and humidity.

Prior to our turn to march around the Bird's Nest track, we had to wait in the holding area, located in another, nearby arena. The coaching staff and I found seats in the very top row of the stadium. It was uncomfortably hot and we were sweating like crazy. After sitting there for a few minutes, LeBron came through one of the stadium portals and motioned for us coaches to come down to where he was. "Come on," he told us. "You guys are going to die up here. We found a better spot."

The players had formed an area on the concourse where the whole team could wait together. And he was right; it was much cooler and more comfortable there. The players did not have to seek us out, there was no expectation of them to do so. But just as they had wanted to join us for dinner in Macau, they wanted us to join them in the more accommodating spot they had found. Sincere care had developed among the members of our team. And it felt great.

TAKE THE TIME

Take the time to form relationships. In granting your team members the time to bond, you establish a foundation of communication, trust, and respect in the way you deal with one another. When your relationships grow from this foundation, you also develop genuine care. If your team can develop this on a personal level, business operations will run more efficiently and you will have a much better chance of reaching your goal.

These strong relationships may not develop fully in a working environment. Your team should have opportunities to relate outside of the office, chances to incorporate humor, and to get to know each others' families. But whether in the boardroom or at a team dinner, I believe that face-to-face communication is absolutely essential. It is how you ensure that you are on the same page and moving forward together.

Unfortunately, in their haste to accomplish their mission, many leaders sometimes forget that relationships can be the most fundamental ingredient for success. In developing these strong bonds, your team will share a uniquely satisfying experience. The friendships that last beyond the completion of your mission are your ultimate reward.

TIME TO DEVELOP A
SUPPORT SYSTEM

To perform at their best, every individual on a team also needs the relationships that comprise their own individual support systems. This may be family, friends, staff, or coworkers. The leader, in particular, needs this system of support because he needs to be fully invested all the time. Having a strong personal system of support behind you makes it easier to immerse yourself in your team and its mission.

Your individual support system not only allows you to fully invest in your team's mission, but it can also serve as a reminder to you of who you are and what strengths you can bring to that mission. It can help you rely on those strengths even when challenges cause you to question yourself.

Hopefully you form strong enough relationships on your team to allow for the development of genuine care, but your family and friends care about you most of all. It brings a great feeling of confidence to know that there are people who are going to support you regardless the outcome of your team's efforts. If you then bring that confidence with you to the work you do with your team, it will help ensure that your teammates are receiving the very best you have to offer.

Moment: My Coach Visits Training Camp—
August 19, 2007—Las Vegas, Nevada

During our training camp prior to the Americas Championship in 2007, the team and I had a very special visitor: my coach from West Point and the man who has had the greatest influence on my career, Bob Knight. We had an optional practice that day for the players to go to the gym and get some extra shooting work done. When Coach Knight stopped in, he went over and spoke briefly with Kobe. I do not know everything that was said in that conversation, but I do know that Coach Knight recommended a book to Kobe called *Lone Survivor*, by former Navy SEAL Marcus Luttrell.

The next morning at breakfast, Kobe mentioned to my wife, Mickie, and me that Coach Knight had made this recommendation. Mickie, an avid reader, was extremely curious to discover the message of a book that Bob Knight would recommend to Kobe Bryant. She went out to a bookstore right after breakfast and purchased two copies, one for Kobe and one for herself. *Lone Survivor* is the powerful, true story of the author's heroic survival of a reconnaissance mission in Afghanistan in which three of his fellow SEALs had been killed. Coach Knight must have believed that Kobe also had a warrior's spirit when it came to playing the game of basketball and that the incredible story of courage, sacrifice, and patriotism could serve as an inspiration for him.

Coach Knight also found some time to spend with me and he gave me the advice that helped me the most over my remaining two summers as national coach. He did not offer me any insights on X's and O's or motivational tactics, then the team wouldn't be my own. He gave me one solitary piece of advice. "Just remember Mike," he said, "you are as good as they are."

I had to laugh. I had been a solid player at West Point, but nowhere close to the level of the guys I was coaching.

"No, I'm serious," he clarified. "*What I'm saying is that you are as good at what you do as they are at what they do.*"

He got his message across. He wanted me to go in with the confidence that I needed to coach this team of stars. As a college coach, I like to think that I help boys become men. But I did sometimes question what I had to offer to this group, who were already men and had found much success in the NBA. Coach Knight knew that I had accepted the biggest challenge of my career. A challenge of this magnitude can bring about fear, and that fear can change you. My coach wanted to ensure that would not happen to me. His support encouraged me to be myself even in the face of this new challenge.

Moment: My Brother and Family Come to the FIBA Americas Championship—August 31, 2007— Las Vegas, Nevada

I invited my family to Las Vegas for our FIBA Americas Championship semifinals and finals, including my brother, Bill; his wife, Pat; and their daughters, Cherisse and Lynette. It meant the world to me to have my big brother there, along with my immediate family, to watch our team qualify to compete in the Olympic Games. Growing up, I always looked up to my big brother and, together, we admired the resolve and dignity of our Polish parents and grandparents. I knew how much it meant to him that I would be coaching a United States team in the Olympics.

When they joined us, I had a meeting with my team in which I discussed the importance of a support system, what having my family there meant to me, and what level of support they could feel from their own families. It was also important to me to let my team know that it would not be a distraction having them around. Far from it, having my immediate and extended family with me helps keep me focused on the task at hand. The people at Duke were accustomed to my wife and daughters being at games, practices, trips, team functions, and recruiting dinners. They came to know over the years that they are a major part of what I do. I just wanted my US team to know that my family was going to be a big part of this challenge as well and that it would make me a better coach having them around. I also wanted them to know that I was comfortable with their family and friends being a part of our team, too.

"It's important to have people around that care about you," I told the team. "When you are trying to accomplish something special, having those close to you around allows them to share in your moments, which then become their moments, too. Your support system can become the other half of your team."

This was also my way of helping my team understand that they weren't just playing for themselves. Of course, we had already talked about the fact that we were playing for our country and for the game of basketball, but we were also very fortunate to be the representatives of our families in this effort. "We are the lucky ones," I said to them. "Not every Bryant or Anthony or Redd or Boeheim will have the chance to participate in something like this, but you do. You come into this as a representative for your entire family."

Our families were going to be around, and we each wanted and needed them there to provide us with support. As a leader, if I excluded them from what we were trying to do, I would have put those families and my players in a bad position because I would have been setting the families up to be a distraction. Those outside support systems should never be made to feel like they have to compete with the team. Having them be a part of things is a benefit to everyone.

Moment: Moe's E-mail to Mickie—July 16, 2008—Durham, North Carolina

Shortly before I was set to leave for training camp and the Olympics, my wife received an e-mail from Moe Mlynski, who's been my best friend since I was six years old. Moe is one of the members of a group of friends I had growing up in Chicago that we called "the Columbos" because we used to play sports together in Columbus schoolyard. We were not a gang. We were just a group of great friends. Since those days, Moe and the Columbos have supported me in all that I have done. They have been there for many of my victories and have comforted me in some of my worst defeats.

There was one Columbo who was almost as close to me as Moe—his name was Rich Glosniak, but we just called him Dicker. Likely both the biggest and smartest of the Columbos, Dicker was a football and basketball player at Weber High School while I was a basketball player there. I was the vice president of our class and Dicker was the secretary. After graduation he went on to play football at Northwestern. I can remember nights when it was just Moe, Dicker, Mickie, and me playing cards all night. Sadly, Dicker passed away in 1995, but we have never forgotten him. And before I left for the greatest challenge of my career, Moe wanted me to know that he, Dicker, and the rest of the Columbos were all with me.

Moe's e-mail to Mickie said that we would be receiving an overnight package the next day. "It contains a remembrance I have from Dicker," he wrote. "His Weber High School football pin. I was wondering if you could take it with you to the Olympics and have it symbolize us there with you in Beijing. We are all with you in Heart and Spirit and want you to know how proud we are of you taking on this endeavor." He concluded his e-mail with a wish that was uniquely Moe, one that he had wished for me many times through the years: "May your team score many and foul few."

I became who I am by being associated with Moe, Dicker, and the Columbos. I learned about real friendship and loyalty from them. Moe's message to me was a reminder that I had the strength of their support behind me and to never forget the things that I learned many years ago on that schoolyard in Chicago.

Moment: Wojo, Chris, and Johnny Travel with Us to China—July 26, 2008—San Jose, California

What put me at ease the most when transitioning from being a college coach to being in charge of a team made up of top pro players was having my Duke staff with me for the ride. Over the course of the three years, Johnny Dawkins, my former Duke associate head coach and now the head coach at Stanford, served as player development coordinator. Though Steve Wojciechowski and Chris Collins, my current Duke associate head coaches, did not hold official titles, they worked extremely hard for USA Basketball in each of the three summers, scouting and helping to run our team practices. For the first two summers, Mike Schrage, my former director of basketball operations at Duke and a current assistant coach at Stanford, joined us as video coordinator. When Mike was unable to come with us for the Olympics in 2008, our new video coordinator at Duke, Kevin Cullen, came on board. I was also given assistance by my new Duke director of basketball operations and son-in-law, Chris Spatola, who helped out with practice and video sessions.

As a college coach leading professional players, I knew I had to start from scratch in a lot of ways. Having my Duke staff around provided me with familiarity, a level of comfort that would not have been there otherwise. When I asked Wojo weeks later how he felt about his experience, one of the things he said was, "A lot of people could have done scouting for you, or made highlight tapes, or run drills, but Chris and I know that no one else could have provided the level of comfort for you that we did. You had your basketball family with you, and I hope you know that we had your back."

I absolutely knew that those guys had my back. Throughout my time as national coach and, in particular, our time in Beijing, I was like a quarterback who never got sacked. They not only helped immensely with our Olympic team's preparation but they also protected my time by constantly checking on how things were going at Duke. They were my offensive line, allowing me to keep focused. When I would ask those guys "Anything to worry about back home?" they would inevitably say no. If I wanted more updates on our players or recruits or anything else at Duke, they provided it. But they instinctively knew where my head needed to be. It also helped a great deal to know that I had staff back home in whom I had the utmost confidence, including my executive administrative assistant, Gerry Brown, and Duke's senior associate athletic director, Mike Cragg.

Moment: My Family Arrives in Beijing—
August 6, 2008—Beijing, China

I have been able to devote so much of myself to my teams over the years because of the support of my family. But this is not something that just happens naturally. When you are completely engrossed in what you do, there is always the potential that your family will resent your career, feeling that it gets the best part of you. I have always tried to keep my family completely involved in what I do and I have found that it pays off, not only in their lives but in mine.

Believe it or not, when all twelve of them arrived in Beijing—my wife, my three daughters, their husbands, and my five grandchildren—it was only then that I could fully throw myself into my team. Imagine that: feeling *more* focused when your family arrives. It wasn't the arrival of a new set of distractions, it was the rest of my team joining me. And I never had to worry about them. They were right there with me so I wasn't thinking about if Lindy was doing okay or if Joey was doing well in school or if Michael had won his football game, or how little Quin was doing. And throughout their nineteen-day trip to China, my family was able to experience some pretty incredible things: attending our basketball games as well as several other Olympic sporting events, visiting and having a family photo taken at the Great Wall of China, and touring the Forbidden City, the Summer Palace, and Tiananmen Square. When a career is truly shared, a family never feels as if it has to compete. In Beijing I was able to go completely into my bubble because I have a great staff and a great family, and so many of them were literally there with me.

Moment: Duke Athletic Director Kevin White Arrives in Beijing—August 18, 2008—Beijing, China

Having several members of my Duke staff with me in Beijing helped keep me focused, but really the support I had from my entire Duke family was incredible. Prior to our leaving for the summer of 2008, the athletic department staff arranged for a huge banner to hang over a major four-lane street near campus, which read "Coach K—Best of Luck in the 2008 Olympics" and had the Duke and USA Basketball logos on either side. I saw it every day on my way to the office and on my way home.

It had been an interesting spring for Duke Athletics, and it had included the hiring of a new athletic director in Dr. Kevin White. Mickie and I had dinner with the Whites a couple times before we left town for the summer. We found out immediately that the four of us would become great friends. I was so pleased when Kevin told me that he was going to make the trip to Beijing to watch our team compete for the Olympic gold.

Kevin had already been in Beijing for three or four days before I even saw him. Sean Ford was the one who told me on one of our bus rides that my athletic director was there and that Sean had tried to encourage him to speak with me in our team meeting room. "No," Kevin had told Sean. "He needs to be focused on what he's doing. I'm not going to bother him. Just let him know that I'm here." Kevin was not there to be seen by me. He was there to represent Duke and show his support for our mission.

When I returned home and saw Kevin at Duke, one of the first things I said to him was, "With eight minutes to go in that gold-medal game, could you believe the look on Kobe's face? What an amazing competitor."

"I didn't see it," he replied. "I was focused on you." Even though Kevin White and I had met prior to his hire at Duke, we had not yet been on the same team. He had never seen me in action as a coach and I had never seen him in action as an AD. His making the trip all the way to China to give his encouragement in our Olympic endeavor cemented a relationship for future challenges that we will face together at Duke. What an incredible act of support from my new boss.

TAKE THE TIME

Take the time to develop a support system. Realize that no matter what it is, you don't have to do it alone. Feeling alone is a scary thing. *But allowing those who have helped you along the way to make you stronger in the moment brings about confidence.* Knowing that I had people like my family, like Moe and Dicker, like Kevin White, Gerry Brown, Chris, Wojo, and Johnny meant that I wasn't just in this thing by myself.

Take the time to emphasize the importance of individual support systems to your team. If they are able to share the experience with their loved ones, they will have an easier time sharing the emotion of it with one another. When people feel alone, they have the tendency to put up walls. *When you feel alone, you act alone.* But when you go onstage knowing that there are people in the audience who will cheer no matter what, you feel a tremendous sense of security. You are able to proceed with the confidence you need to be yourself. You want your entire team to be able to act with this kind of confidence.

Include your established system of support in the pursuit of your mission because it will allow you to share the outcome in the end, no matter what that outcome may be. If you should fail, the support system is the cushion that you fall back on. They are the ones who will always be there, the ones who will help you turn the failure into a learning experience. And if you succeed, sharing that moment makes it feel even better. You share the moment with your team when it occurs, and then you can share it time and time again with the family and friends who were with you, who were able to be a part of your team, too.

TIME TO ESTABLISH
STANDARDS

*I*n *developing teams, I don't believe in rules. I believe in stan-dards. Rules don't promote teamwork, standards do.* Rules are issued by a leader to a group, and the group can either follow those rules or break them. When something is presented as a rule, you can't own it. You can't live it. Standards, on the other hand, are lived. This is what we do all the time. These are the things for which we hold one another accountable. A team needs to work together to develop its particular set of standards. This process itself promotes teamwork. And when standards are established as a part of a group effort, they are understood and are capable of being embraced on a deeper level.

A major part of becoming a team, then, is the establishment and collective acceptance of *your* standards, based on your team's makeup and centered on your unique goal. Once a group of in-dividuals formulates and agrees to their standards, they become united, single-minded in purpose. Standards are not the things that we ought to do, they are simply the things that we already do—they comprise who we are. Imagine being on a team where you never have to fake it, where you can always be yourself and you can always be real. In my experience I have found that often the simplest and most fundamental things are not said. But standards should never go unspoken.

Moment: Our Standards Meeting—July 20, 2008— Las Vegas, Nevada

Our team and staff had just gathered in Las Vegas for our first team meeting and practice as the United States Olympic basketball team. Behind us were two years of preparation, learning the international game and establishing our internal relationships. Ahead of us was the last leg of our journey. This was an extremely important moment for our team—this was *the* meeting.

Appropriately, it was Jerry Colangelo who addressed the team first. USA Basketball's one-man committee spoke briefly, reminding us all that this whole thing began in December 2005, when he first met with Carmelo Anthony in Washington, D.C., and then LeBron James in Chicago. "This moment seemed like a long way off then," he said, "but it's here." Coming from humble roots, Jerry has achieved success in every level of sport. "But nothing," he told us, "could be quite like winning gold." In what Jerry called his "last welcome" for this team, he reminded all of us that this was the culmination of our journey. Now it was time to get the job done.

When it was my turn to address the team, I began by reminding them of our plans for the week. These were professional players, so I always made a conscious effort to let them know exactly what was going on. No surprises. I also continually asked them for their feedback on scheduling, practice, and any other plans. If something wasn't working, we obviously wanted to fix it. *Leaders should remember that not all the good ideas have to come from the top, and they should be secure enough to change plans based on the input of the team.* Why would you have formed a team in the first place if you could do it all on your own?

Next, I told them that we were going to distribute notebooks and include in them some documents that would be of the utmost

importance to us for the next six weeks. I believe in visual rein-
forcement; things take on new meaning when you can actually
see them in front of you. I told the guys, "You have to know what
you're going for and sometimes you have to see it." The first page
of our notebooks would be a full-page picture of an Olympic
gold medal, an image that would be displayed on the large screen
of our meeting room every time we met. "That's our goal. And
we want you to see it every day; we're going to look at it every
day." I pointed to the gold medal on the screen and emphasized,
"And that's *ours*." You share a lot when you are on a team, but
the primary thing that you share is your common goal. Ours was
Olympic gold.

"Whenever you are going towards a destination," I continued,
"you have to have a road map. How do you get there?" The second page of our notebooks would be the Olympic bracket—the
schedule of the games we would play—our path to the gold-
medal game.

There was one more document that needed to be included. But
the staff and I could not create this one on our own; we needed
to develop it together as a team. It was time for us to define our
standards and to put them on paper so that, like our goal and our
road map, we could see them every day.

I started by presenting two standards that are vital to the formation of relationships, two concepts that are fundamental to a team
dynamic: communication and trust. I said to my guys, "When we
talk to each other, we look each other in the eye, we tell each
other the truth, and we treat each other like men." As a result
of this honest and respectful communication, we would develop
trust. "So if you tell me something or if I tell you something or if
any of the coaching staff tells you something, I know you trust us
and we trust you. I don't know how we can get beat if we communicate and trust and we set other good standards."

Prior to our standards meeting, I had met individually with
Dwyane, Kobe, LeBron, and Jason. I knew that this upcoming

team meeting would set the tone for the rest of our time together. I knew it had to go well. To be a good builder of teams, you need to identify these crucial moments and take the necessary measures to ensure that they accomplish what you intend. Separately, I told each of these four guys that we were going to have a team meeting about how we would live on a day-to-day basis. I let them know that I planned to open it up to the players and staff for input. "I need you to speak," I told them. "Say anything you want to say. But say something. And speak from the heart."

You cannot assume that people are automatically going to speak up. But by making certain that someone will, you create an atmosphere conducive to contributions from everyone. The fact that I had these individual meetings prior to the team meeting does not mean I told them to say what I wanted to hear. It's not about that. It's about making sure that you fully prepare for impact moments the right way. If we are having a team meeting for the specific purpose of developing *team* standards and no one speaks, those standards take on the appearance of rules. You have to give your team the opportunity to contribute to your collective identity. And they did.

So, after I had suggested communication and trust as two of our standards, I opened it up to everyone for input. "It can't be my standards, or Jerry's, or Deron's, or Michael's; it's got to be all of ours," I said.

Jason Kidd spoke first, reiterating a point that he had made the previous summer. "I think being on time is going to be huge," he said. I agreed completely. Being on time is a sign of respect for your teammates and coaches and for your task. But respect entailed more than that for our team. Elaborating on Jason's point, I said that we would be respectful of each other but also respectful of our opponents in preparing the right way. Respect was added to the list of our gold standards.

Next, Dwyane Wade spoke. Though he had joined us in Las Vegas the previous summer and sat with us on the bench for our final two FIBA Americas Championship games, Dwyane had been unable to play because of his injury. Like most great competitors, he was extremely frustrated by this. For his voice to be one of those heard at our standards meeting put him right back in the middle of things where he belonged. Anyone who watched our team play in the Olympics knows how indispensible he was.

Dwyane was also one of the four members of our 2008 Olympic team who had been on the bronze-medal-winning team in the 2004 Olympics, the team that had become known far better for losing the gold than winning the bronze. Dwyane, Carlos, Carmelo, and LeBron had carried that burden for four years. In some respects these guys, more than the others, had something to prove, something to reclaim. Dwyane spoke of having a commitment to each person. For him, this was something that had been missing four years earlier. "I think it's about being committed to one another," he said, "and making sure we have each other's backs. No matter what." What Dwyane was talking about was the concept of collective responsibility, which I define with the phrase, "we win and we lose together." This would be another standard.

Kobe Bryant spoke next: "No matter where you play—if you're playing here, if you're playing on Mars—if you can shut somebody down and rebound the basketball, you're going to win no matter who you're playing against. And I think that's a standard that we have to set." Kobe believed that our team needed to have a joint focus on defense and rebounding, something not typically associated with NBA All-Star play. "I think when they look at us, they see guys that are talented and explosive offensively, but they don't think that we have the guts to lock down defensively and rebound the ball. In knowing a lot of guys who play overseas, that's what they think about us. They think we're a bunch of showboat players who score a lot of points and do a lot of things offensively but won't do the dirty work to win." In playing great defense, Kobe believed that he and his teammates could rid the world of a common misconception about NBA stars.

In response to Kobe's point, I told the team that I believed great defense on our part was the key to the whole endeavor. "I'm sixty-one years old, and this will be my thirty-fourth year as a head coach," I told them. "You dream of winning a gold medal, an NBA championship, an NCAA championship. But really for this next thirty-five days, I'm going to live my dream and have this become the greatest team to ever play defense on this planet. This is not *the* Dream Team, but it could be a dream team for defense.

"We have so many weapons," I continued. "We have the three best point guards in the world. Can't we pick our opponents up at three-quarter court and dog them? You don't have to pace yourselves. We've got the best center in the world, the best shot-blocker, the strongest guy. And we have the greatest athletes on the perimeter of any team that has ever played basketball." If we could harness all of that talent and ability, we could gamble on defense and we could play to exhaustion, because we knew we had each other's backs. Defense would become another standard to which we would hold one another accountable.

When Michael Redd spoke next, he talked about having a "special hunger." He told our team, "I get asked all the time, 'Who's going to be the toughest team that you play?' and I say, 'All of them.' It's not going to just be Argentina or Spain. I'm looking at every team as a challenge. Hunger." Michael was talking about having a standard of performance. As a team, we needed to play every possession.

I added to that, "No bad practices. No bad games. We only have thirty-five days together; can't we make every one of them a good day?" When the lifetime of your season is thirty-five days as opposed to several months, time is even more precious. Every minute counts. If you don't prepare to win, you don't deserve to win. We had to hold ourselves to a level of hunger in our performance that made us worthy of winning. This was another gold standard that we added to our team's list.

Nate McMillan then brought up one of his key words for our

team, saying that we needed to be "connected" on both ends of the floor. He specifically brought up defense against a pick-and-roll, which is the most difficult offensive play to defend in basketball and would become a focus of our team defense. "But I think if we're connected," Coach McMillan said, "if we communicate and we're connected, we can defend anything they put out on the floor." Being connected as a unit means being unselfish. It's not about me, it's about us. If we look at it this way, we should have fun playing as a team on offense and on defense.

Being unselfish and connected also means that each member of the team should be comfortable with their role. With regard to playing time, I told the team, "There's no way I can satisfy what you would normally want." But this was not a normal situation. "We've got to do this differently. And I hope you know me well enough by now to know that I'll talk to any of you face-to-face, I'll try to keep explaining your roles. There can't be any 'stuff' where you don't think I believe in you or you wonder what the staff and I are doing. That can't happen. Let's be unselfish and be connected."

Related to being connected and being unselfish is being flexible. Our team was a collection of men who were All-Stars in their own right, who were franchise players on their NBA teams, who regularly played forty-plus minutes a game. But each player had to become flexible to coexist on a team that had twelve stars instead of only one or two. The ability to be flexible also needed to manifest itself in the way we related to officials. I asked our team to be strong, to show no weakness, and to never complain about a call. Unselfishness and flexibility became our standards as well.

I couldn't let the meeting end without adding to the list three more standards that have been an essential part of the character of all my teams: care, enthusiasm, and pride. Care for one another is the way we show each other and the world that we are brothers; it's what develops over the course of our bonding and forming strong relationships. If a teammate is knocked down, we pick him up. When one of us makes a great play, we all celebrate.

When one of us has a bad game, we remind him of our collective responsibility.

Enthusiasm is a natural remedy for pressure. We cannot forget to have fun. How often will we get to play with this caliber of talent?

And in this endeavor, pride was a no-brainer. We were playing for our country. We were headed to the Olympics. I had never been more proud.

In concluding the meeting, I invoked an analogy I commonly use: the fist. Five guys playing as one, like a fist instead of five outstretched fingers, are stronger than any of us could ever be individually. As I spoke to my team and formed a fist, I looked down at my hand and saw the ring I was awarded as an assistant coach with the 1992 Dream Team. It was fortuitous that it caught my eye because it gave me the perfect way to conclude that meeting. I looked down at my ring and said, "This ring is a reminder to me of guys being committed, but also a reminder of winning. But you know what? This ring is sixteen years old. I want a new ring. Tonight is the last night I'm going to wear it because the next ring I wear and that every one of you guys are going to wear is the 2008 Olympic gold-medal ring." I joked with them, "Unless you're really obnoxious, you are not going to walk around wearing your gold medal. But you will wear that ring."

Wrapping up, I said to them, "You know what I want the new ring to be a reminder of? Of the brotherhood and the commitment and the fact that we had a goal, a destination, we followed the road map, and we had standards. You'll remember that for the rest of your lives."

I thought that could have ended the meeting pretty darn well, but it was another voice that would provide the meeting's perfect conclusion. When LeBron James spoke, everyone was silent. "I think we've got to be a no-excuse team," he said. "When we go across these waters and we go play, we've got to be a no-excuse team. What I mean is, it's going to be us against the world, and we've got to look at it that way. We can't blame the refs, we can't blame the crowd, we can't blame anything else on anybody. We're in a position right now where we control our own destiny." LeBron confessed that he was sometimes guilty of feeling like he could win an NBA championship if he had Dwight Howard on his team, or Carlos Boozer, or if he had Chris Paul as his point guard. He said that this team had everything they had always dreamed of individually, being surrounded by that level of player.

Looking around the room at his teammates, LeBron asked, "What's my excuse now? I've got all of you on this team. So, what's my excuse now?" His words built momentum as he spoke: "This is everything we've always dreamed of, having that guy next to you and winning something. That gold medal is what we've all been dreaming about. I'm excited. And I know you guys are. This is what I've always wanted, playing alongside Carmelo, playing alongside Jason, and playing with Kobe. We don't have an excuse now. None of us." LeBron's point would be put at the top of our list of gold standards: no excuses. With no way to improve upon his words, I concluded with "Amen. Well said."

The third document was added to our notebooks. It was entitled "Gold Standards," incorporating what each of the players had said in our meeting. This was a list of what we, as a team, would always do. This was the way we would live for the next thirty-five days.

GOLD STANDARDS

What we do all the time and what we hold each other accountable for:

1. NO EXCUSES
   - We have what it takes to win.
2. GREAT DEFENSE
   - This is the key to winning the gold.
   - We do the dirty work.

3. COMMUNICATION
- We look each other in the eye.
- We tell each other the truth.

4. TRUST
- We believe in each other.

5. COLLECTIVE RESPONSIBILITY
- We are committed to each other.
- We win together.

6. CARE
- We have each other's backs.
- We give aid to a teammate.

7. RESPECT
- We respect each other and our opponents.
- We're always on time.
- We're always prepared.

8. INTELLIGENCE
- We take good shots.
- We're aware of team fouls.
- We know the scouting report.

9. POISE
- We show no weakness.

10. FLEXIBILITY
- We can handle any situation.
- We don't complain.

11. UNSELFISHNESS
- We're connected.
- We make the extra pass.
- Our value is not measured in playing time.

12. AGGRESSIVENESS
- We play hard every possession.

13. ENTHUSIASM
- This is fun.

14. PERFORMANCE
    - We're hungry.
    - We have no bad practices.
15. PRIDE
    - We are the best team in the world and we represent the best country.

Moment: USA Basketball Visits the Olympic Village—August 6, 2008—Beijng, China

In addition to living our gold standards in our on-court performance, our players planned to set a new standard for USA Basketball in the way we operated off the basketball court. This meant behaving in a way that would bring honor to ourselves, our country, and our sport. While security issues made it necessary for us to stay in our own hotel along with the women's basketball team away from the Olympic Village, the players wanted our fellow American athletes to know that we recognized ourselves as a part of a larger contingent: Team USA. So the very first night of our arrival, the players arranged to take a bus over to the Village to visit with the other athletes. They spent about four hours there, meeting and mingling and enjoying a McDonald's dinner. It was the college campus atmosphere that three of our players had never experienced and only one player had for a full four years. They loved being there in what Kobe described as "Disney World for athletes."

Our players made a conscious commitment to support other Americans in their respective sports. Jason Kidd went to several beach volleyball matches. LeBron James, Tayshaun Prince, and Chris Paul joined him for the semifinals. LeBron also made a trip to the tennis venue to watch the Williams sisters compete, and was able to meet and spend time with Roger Federer and Rafael Nadal. Dwight Howard supported the US indoor volleyball team. Kobe Bryant, who was an avid soccer player growing up in Italy, attended the women's soccer finals. And Kobe, along with LeBron,

Jason, Chris Paul, and Carmelo Anthony, had the privilege of wit-
nessing the greatness of Michael Phelps in the swimming pool in
four of his eight gold-medal performances.

Like the rest of our country, our players were captivated by Phelps
and they were happy to share the Olympic spotlight with a truly incredible athlete. In a lot of ways, our players felt like Phelps could
understand them and their positions because he was experiencing an
even greater level of scrutiny. Everyone watched Michael Phelps; he
was under enormous pressure. And he wowed them all.

Between events, Phelps's mom took pictures with our players.
Kobe Bryant, maybe the second most popular individual in China
after Yao Ming, asked Phelps to pose for a photo with him. Kobe
later said of Phelps in an interview, "To be honest with you, I don't
think I've ever seen anything more spectacular than the performance they put on in the pool. That's what the Olympics are about
for me, going out and watching greatness."

After our players attended his events, Phelps was quoted as saying, "Having those guys there is pretty special. You can kind of hear
them starting cheers and getting everybody going. It's pretty neat."
After our game against Germany in pool play, something pretty neat
happened for us. Michael Phelps had come to watch us play and
spent time with our team in the locker room afterward. The goodwill
created by our players' having and upholding a set of shared standards was extraordinary to behold.

The residual effects of being good ambassadors for our game
were that our players were able to see and feel the competition. In several cases, they were able to watch Americans being
awarded gold medals. It gave them the opportunity to embrace
the Olympic-caliber emotional impact that competition can have
on athletes. It also served as an example of the way that helping
someone else helps you, too. Our team was seen supporting their
fellow Olympians, and it helped people understand that they were
good guys, that they had a sense of perspective and an appreciation for the Olympic stage.

Chris Sheridan, who covered our team throughout the Games for ESPN.com, said of our players prior to the gold-medal game, "Win or lose Sunday against Spain, the members of Team USA have been golden ambassadors for their country and sport. It happened so many times and in so many ways, no one could possibly count off how many hearts and minds they've won over—both among the Chinese, and among other American athletes."

Sometimes reporters are the greatest skeptics of all, and, no doubt, a lot of coverage of the 2004 team as well as our 2006 team had been cynical about the future of the United States in international basketball. Chris Sheridan is a terrific student of the international game. And while he did not jump on board right away, we earned his respect in much the same way that we earned back international respect. Once people could see that we had studied the international game and held real respect for our opponents and this venue, I believe they truly wanted to see us succeed and were genuinely happy when we did.

Moment: Johnson & Johnson Sponsor Party— August 17, 2008—Beijing, China

One of the most satisfying things about team building is watching as the group's acceptance of your gold standards slowly manifests in the way your team members represent themselves on a daily basis. Over recent years, much has been made of the NBA dress code and the players' seeming unwillingness to cooperate with the league-imposed rules of dress. The coaching staff and I originally wondered if we would have trouble encouraging the players to dress a particular way when representing the United States.

Imagine how proud we were the night of a hospitality function hosted by one of our sponsors, Johnson & Johnson, on the Olympic Green. We had asked that the players and staff dress in collared shirts and slacks. That was all we asked. It was a really good moment when almost every player showed up for the party wearing jackets, ties, or both. They all looked great.

When your team completely embraces the standards that define you, you will begin to see those standards manifested in a shared pride that is reflected in everything you do. Those guys did not show up to that party as individuals, they showed up as members of a team, and as such they chose to represent each other with the utmost class. It was no longer about merely meeting expectations, it was about exceeding them.

Moment: The Duke Standards Meeting— September 25, 2008—Durham, North Carolina

In any business, you can sometimes find yourself a part of more than one team; you may even be the leader of multiple teams. During my three years as the national coach, I also remained the head coach at Duke. I love being the Duke coach. And it was essential that I did not let one team suffer while building another. This meant making a number of changes, including empowering people to help take care of the Duke players during my absence, changing some things around with regard to recruiting schedules, and eliminating some of my other responsibilities, at least temporarily. It was a challenge, but I had a flexible and capable staff at Duke and an understanding and supportive Duke team.

Obviously, the experiences that I have had in thirty-three years as a head coach at West Point and Duke prepared me going into the new challenge with USA Basketball. But I was excited to discover that the USA Basketball experience would make me a better Duke coach. It was a reminder for me of how to adapt and how to change limits. Even more, it was a reminder of how to have fun coaching my team rather than responding to external pressures.

The standards meeting that I had with the US team before we left for China was the foundation for our summer together. We constantly referred back to that meeting. Time and time again we reminded our team of the words they themselves had said and the collective promise that we made. Upon returning to Duke, I knew I had to practice what I preached, and within a week of my return I met with my Duke team to open up the discussion about their standards. In this meeting, I distributed the list of standards the US team devised but told my Duke team that these would not be the same as the ones we would adopt. I just wanted them to see the standards that guided the US team as they began to think about how we would define ourselves.

Before our season began, we produced a list of Duke Standards. These were the things that our 2008–2009 Duke Basketball team would do all the time and the things for which our Duke players and staff would hold one another accountable. What was so interesting to me was comparing their list to the list we devised as an Olympic team. Of course, there was some overlap. Communication and respect, among other things, are standards that should be a part of your list whether you are a basketball team, a business, or a family. Likewise, there are certain things that will be common standards among teams in the same industry, like defense in our case. But the lists were different. Looking at the two lists side by side allowed me to see what I had always believed. Every team is different, and the leader must approach each team with that understanding.

2008–2009 DUKE STANDARDS

1. GREAT DEFENSE AND REBOUNDING
    -   It starts here.
    -   We do the dirty work.
2. CONFIDENCE
    -   We believe in our own abilities.
    -   We believe in each other.
3. CONFRONT IMMEDIATELY
    -   We let nothing linger.

4. COMMUNICATION
   - We look each other in the eye.
   - We tell the truth *immediately*.
5. TRUST
   - We have each other's back.
6. NO EXCUSES
   - We have what we need to win.
7. POISE
   - We have winning faces.
   - We show no weakness.
8. DEPENDABILITY
   - We can be counted on.
9. COLLECTIVE RESPONSIBILITY
   - We win and we lose together.
10. ENTHUSIASM
    - We bring energy every day.
    - No bad practices.
11. RESPECT
    - We are always on time.
    - We prepare for every opponent.
12. FLEXIBILITY
    - We don't complain.
    - We can handle any situation.
13. INTELLIGENCE
    - We take good shots.
    - We are aware of team fouls.
    - We know the scouting report.
14. CARE
    - We give aid to a teammate immediately, on and off the court.
15. AGGRESSIVENESS
    - We play hard every day.
16. REPRESENT OUR PROGRAM OFF THE COURT

17. UNSELFISHNESS
    - We make the extra pass.
    - Our value is not measured in playing time.
18. WE ARE *THIS* DUKE TEAM
    - The time is now—not the past.
19. FAMILY
    - No one is closer.
20. PRIDE
    - We represent the best program and the best school in the country.

TAKE THE TIME

Take the time to establish standards. And take the time to write them down. These standards will define the character of your team. If you choose to have a standards meeting, remember how important it is to have multiple voices bring that meeting to life. It's okay to plan for moments. So many times a little planning goes a long way, and those moments turn out better than you ever anticipated.

In putting together your standards, remember that it is essential to involve your entire team. Standards are not rules issued by the boss; they are a collective identity. Remember, *standards are the things that you do all the time and the things for which you hold one another accountable.* Once complete, your team can look at that list and say, "That's who we are." As you move forward and are challenged by competition and adversity, you can look at your team and simply say, "Let's be ourselves." If you have established standards, they'll know exactly what you mean.

TIME TO CULTIVATE
LEADERSHIP

I think one of the primary mistakes that leaders make in team building is in believing that they have to be the sole provider of leadership. *Great teams have multiple leaders, multiple voices.* A major part of building a team is discovering who those voices will be and cultivating them, making sure that their leadership is established within your group. In order to do this, the team leader must first make certain that he or she has a solid relationship with those leaders. All members of the team should be bonded to one another but a leader must be connected, most of all, with his internal leadership.

A leader has to recognize when he or she has the best feel for a given situation—and when that feel is better felt by someone else. In sport, it is the players who have the best feel for the game once they are out on the court or field of competition. You have to have a trusting relationship with your internal leaders so that you can allow them to guide your team once the game clock has started. It is their feel for the game that should guide the way you coach, as well.

Part of cultivating leadership is ensuring that your team will hear a number of different voices, not the leader's alone. A leader must make a realistic assessment of the attention span of his or her group. Of course, this varies from team to team, and from time to time within your team. I am not the first to point out that attention spans seem to grow shorter and shorter with each generation. It has become increasingly true, then, that no matter who you are or what success you have achieved, there is only a finite period of time during which you can speak and expect a group to listen. There is a window.

Let's say, for example, that you feel your team has a fifteen-minute attention-span window. You can personally talk to that team for fifteen good minutes. But when you have established several different voices on your team, you can open that window a little more by utilizing those other voices. My basketball team may only be able to listen to me for fifteen minutes, but I can get more time out of a meeting by having Coach D'Antoni address them about offense, or Jason Kidd emphasize respect, or LeBron James tell us that we won't make excuses. The window can also be opened through the use of other media. Sights and sounds can create interest among your team while still getting across your intended message.

There are other reasons to establish these voices on your team. One is simply this: someone may be able to express something much better than you or communicate it in a way that really connects with the team. For example, our standards meeting found its ideal conclusion in the words spoken by LeBron. Nothing I could have said would have brought that meeting to a better or stronger close. A leader doesn't have an exclusive contract on getting a point across. You have to have enough confidence in your leadership to share it. And really, this will make your team respect you more because they will be able to perceive your level of security. If you can make clear that it doesn't always have to be *yours*, you can more deeply ingrain the understanding that it is *ours*.

If you think about it, it's really simple. If you win, what does it matter who said what? Why wouldn't you want things to be delivered in the best way possible?

Though our Duke teams vote on and name captains every season, we did not officially name captains of our national team. We
found that the most effective way to develop leadership among
this group of men and professional players was to allow it to
emerge. During our time together, the leadership of our team assumed their roles, and the three players who came to stand out as
my internal leadership were completely accepted by their teammates and valued by the coaching staff. LeBron James, Kobe Bryant, and Jason Kidd were the guys who I always went to when I
needed to feel the pulse of the team or when I wanted to get a
message across to the group. I never had to ask them twice to get
something done. They were completely committed to the group,
to me, and to our mission.

LEBRON JAMES MOMENTS

Going into my first summer as the national coach in 2006, I was
nervous. I had been a head coach for thirty-one years already, and
I had been in basketball nearly my whole life, so this nervousness
was a strange feeling for me. But I was also excited. I knew I was
going to get to coach one of the most talented teams in the history
of basketball. What lover of the game wouldn't be excited—and
nervous?

I did not know LeBron James well going in. I knew he had
matchless talent. I knew he would be a major factor in trying to
bring back the gold medal. But what I knew about LeBron then
does not scratch the surface of what I know now. I had no idea
how smart he is, what a tremendous leader he is, and how important our relationship with one another would be to this whole
endeavor. Undoubtedly, people can recognize that LeBron and
I come from two different worlds, and one can imagine that we
likely had many preconceived notions of who the other might be.
LeBron knew that I was a West Point graduate and that I had been
the head coach at Duke for a long time. He likely believed that I

was a straight-laced guy with little sense of humor. Strict, maybe. Inflexible, most likely. LeBron had made the career choice to forgo college and go directly to the NBA, so he had never had a relationship with a college coach. And with the success he had achieved already in his career, he probably never needed one. And yet, here we were: the college coach and the young pro phenom.

In the summer of 2006, I decided to have several short, individual meetings with LeBron with the intention of making him aware of how important he was to this mission. That summer was when I first recognized LeBron's profound intelligence. During our long trips to China, South Korea, and Japan, our players often played cards to pass the hours. At times I would observe them, and I noticed that LeBron played cards differently than most. He was always talking and following the action of the game better than the others. He was in complete control. He kept the game organized, he kept it moving. He knew what the next move would be before any other player at the table. It was in watching LeBron play cards that I began to see something special in him aside from his obvious physical gifts. After a few minutes, I couldn't help but interrupt, "You know what, LeBron?" I said. "I think you're pretty damn smart."

LeBron smiled back at me and agreed, saying, "Yeah, Coach, maybe I should have applied to Duke." It was a simple moment. It was brief. It was even humorous. But, most important, it was a mutual display of respect. I let him know that I saw him for the intelligent player he was. And he made it clear to me and to his teammates that he had respect for who I was as a college coach.

One thing that was also clear about LeBron from the beginning was that he was a great entertainer. I enjoyed his sense of humor, but even more than that I loved his charisma. He automatically attracted people to him. You found yourself wanting to be around LeBron because you knew you would enjoy yourself and that you would be energized.

As soon as I knew these things about LeBron, I wanted to cultivate his leadership on our team. But, honestly, I think I may have asked too much of him that first summer. I asked him to do things that he might not have been quite ready to do or perhaps that he needed more internal support to accomplish. LeBron was still learning about himself as a player, me as a coach, our offensive and defensive systems, and the international game. He had a lot on his plate.

The loss to Greece in the semifinals of the FIBA World Championship made us all take a step back and examine ourselves more closely. One thing that I recognized immediately was that our relationships weren't strong enough to support the type of communication that you need from the bench to the court and vice versa. Before playing Argentina for the bronze medal of the World Championships, I asked for a meeting with LeBron, the team's strongest voice and most magnetic leader.

Of course, we were both devastated by the previous night's loss. So, in our meeting I told him that we were going to make a couple of changes for the Argentina game. One of the primary changes was that LeBron would be our starter at point guard. This is the position typically associated with the most coach-to-player communication in basketball. So, in doing this, I was sending a message. LeBron James was **going** to be my leader on the court.

A lot of people wanted us to fail. They wanted to call him "LeBronze" and say he wasn't worthy of being a champion. I wanted him to know that I understood who he was and what he was capable of doing. "We need you in order to win this game," I told him. "We need you to lead us. We need you to show great enthusiasm. Can you do that?" I asked.

He looked me right in the eye and simply said, "I can do that."

And I believed him. After our loss to Greece, coming back and winning that bronze-medal game against a very talented Argentina team was an enormous feat. We showed the world that we understood there were still things that we needed to learn but that we were not going away. LeBron led us in that victory. It was a huge moment both in our personal relationship and for the future of our team.

The next summer our team would come together again for

training and participation in the 2007 FIBA Americas Championship. We would need to place either first or second in this tournament to qualify for the Olympic Games the following summer.
Prior to assembling as a team in Las Vegas in July, LeBron hosted
an event in Akron, Ohio, in June for all his corporate sponsors. He
called and asked if I would come to Akron and speak to the group
as a kickoff for the conference. I knew it would be a time for us
to grow closer and I jumped at the opportunity.

The speech went well, and I think it got the conference off to a
good start. But the part of the trip that I will always think back on is
a dinner we had following my talk. Seated at our table were LeBron,
his closest friends and advisors, and me. For the next few hours, I
became a part of LeBron's family. We talked about everything, from
our upcoming challenge that summer, to his Cleveland Cavaliers
team, to my Duke team, to the state of basketball in general. And
we had fun. We goofed on one another. LeBron laughed at my
jokes and I laughed at his. It was one of those moments in which
you know you have really connected with someone at a new level.
We got to know each other so much better over that one meal, we
realized that we truly liked each other, and we began to really trust
that relationship. He invited me in. And it was crucial to the future
of our team that I accepted his invitation. *In team building, it is vital
to recognize the need for moments like these, moments that may
never come about as the result of a formal meeting.*

Because the meal was going so well, I also wanted to use it as
an opportunity to find out what LeBron thought of our team since
we had made some changes from the previous summer. There
would be new faces: Kobe Bryant, Jason Kidd, Michael Redd, and
Tayshaun Prince. "What do you think of the new guys?" I asked
him. "How do you think they will fit in?"

You could tell he was excited. "I really like J Kidd," he said.
"I think he is the best passer in the game. He sees things and instantly reacts." He went on: "I love to pass and I can see things,
too, but I want to learn to see things the way he sees them."

"And what about Kobe?" I asked.

"Kobe prepares better than anyone," LeBron answered. "I want to learn from the way he works." So much has been made of how to get these All-Star egos to sacrifice in order to become part of a true team. LeBron already understood a lot about what it takes. In part, it's making the members of your team realize that by being a part of a group, they can become better individually. Remember, becoming part of a team is not all about sacrifice. He knew that there were things he could learn from Jason and Kobe, just as they could learn from him. They could all make each other better.

When we convened as a team in July 2007, I loved watching how LeBron and Jason Kidd did everything together: they sat together at team meetings, they went out together, they even took the early team bus to every game to get in extra shooting before game time. I also loved watching how LeBron and Kobe's relationship developed. There is a certain earnestness about Kobe; it is part of what makes him great. But LeBron was able to joke with him and bring out a lighter side. The relationships among the players were critical, just as critical as my relationships with them.

After we won the FIBA Americas Championship and earned our ticket to Beijing, LeBron and I kept in touch throughout the year and followed each other's respective seasons. LeBron called me after I won my 800th game as a head coach in early March and let me know he thought that was "pretty good, Coach." He also called me before our last regular season game against North Carolina. He wanted to apologize because he had planned to surprise me by showing up for the game, but a snowstorm in Ohio had prevented him from doing so. Still, I knew I had his support. I wrote him a couple times throughout the year and gave him a call when the Cavaliers were headed to the NBA Playoffs.

As the playoffs began, I received a phone call from Danny Ferry, a former player of mine at Duke who was now the general manager of the Cleveland franchise. He had been walking through the Cleveland locker room and, out of the corner of his eye, noticed a letter in LeBron's locker. It caught his attention because the letterhead had a Duke emblem on it, a symbol with which Danny was very familiar but seemed out of context in his Cavaliers' locker room. He stepped a little closer and saw that it was a letter from me. "I'm so glad that you and LeBron have that relationship," Danny told me. "I was hoping that would happen. And it makes me feel so good to see that it did." If, like many teams, you have breaks between your time together, it is vital that you not take a step backward in your individual relationships. You may not be able to come together and practice or watch film during these breaks, but you can continue building your team by cultivating those relationships, and particularly those with your team's internal leaders.

Prior to our Olympic team coming together for our final training camp in July 2008, I had the opportunity to be with LeBron again when I was on the road recruiting for my Duke team. LeBron hosts a skills camp in Akron every summer that is attended by some of the top high school prospects. I was watching the action on the court from my seat in the stands when LeBron walked into the gym. His eyes found me immediately and, as I stood to come over to him, he motioned for me to remain seated. Despite all of the people in the gym who wanted LeBron's attention, he came directly over to me, sat down, and we spent some time talking. Reminiscent of my words to him before our bronze-medal game in 2006, I said to him, "We need you to be a leader this summer. I am really going to rely on you."

LeBron leaned in closer to me and said, "Coach, this is a huge time for USA Basketball. We need to win *now*. You can ask me to do anything, and I'll do it. Anything you ask, Coach, you can count on me." By now, I was 100 percent confident in my relationship with LeBron and so was he. I knew that these words, coming out of the mouth of one of the top players in the world, were going to mean amazing things for our Olympic team and for the future of USA Basketball.

Often in team building, you can get someone on your team who is recognized as the most talented individual, and the leader may be envious of or feel intimidated by that person. A leader has to realize that he is not always the best, most talented, or smartest one in the room. But that leader must also realize that he or she darn well better have a great relationship with whoever that person is if the team is to be successful—a relationship without jealousy, built on trust and communication, and where you know that you can count on one another.

One more moment with LeBron that will stay with me for the rest of my life was a talk I had with him the day before our Olympic gold-medal game against Spain. I just felt I wanted to connect with him once more, coach to player, one-on-one, before our ultimate moment of truth. "LeBron," I said, "I know you are going to be nervous tomorrow. I'm going to be nervous tomorrow. It's the biggest game that you will have played and the biggest game that I will have coached. Use your voice and your leadership to overcome those nerves. And I want you to know that I am here for you."

People like LeBron and the rest of the guys on our Olympic team have to project a superhuman image. They get a lot for it, but it can still be a very lonely place. I wanted LeBron to know that in our championship moment, he was not alone. I paused and grabbed his arm. "Be yourself," I said. "This will be your first championship. And I want you to know, it is my *honor* to be your coach in your first championship, son." LeBron was quiet in this moment, but he looked at me with a smile and nodded. After the incredible development of our relationship over the past three years, I wanted him to know that it was a privilege for me to have come this far with him and that I felt he could lead us in taking that final step.

People often ask me, "Was LeBron coachable?" My answer is a resounding "Yes!" He was coachable right from the beginning. But once we developed that communication and trust with one another, once we formed a bond, he was beyond coachable; he was incredible. One of the primary things LeBron did for our team was give us energy. He was *on* all the time. In his own entertaining way, LeBron kept everyone going. I love thinking of all the times King James held court with our team: during stretching at the beginning of practice, on our team buses, at team meals. By keeping us loose, he helped us relax and focus.

Even better, because of our connection with one another, I could rely on LeBron to use his humor and personality to sell our concepts to the team. I will always remember the sound of his booming voice, the way everyone in the room turned to look when he walked in for breakfast and shouted out his typical "Good morning, everyone," the way he made us all laugh, and the way he injected energy into the entire team. If a practice was not going well, I could pull LeBron aside and say, "I'm going to need you today." And he would find a way to bring everyone out of the slump. He was the one on our team who could do that the best.

There is no player who grew more over those three years than LeBron James. I have come to love him and I know he feels the same. What a terrific relationship to have with a leader on your team.

KOBE BRYANT MOMENTS

My relationship with Kobe Bryant started many years before my relationship with any of the other players on the team. He was an eighteen-year-old high school senior, and I was recruiting him to come to Duke. I know that had he not chosen to go directly to the NBA, he would have chosen to play his college career for me. But when he chose to enter the NBA draft and became a Los Angeles Laker, I missed out on my first opportunity to coach Kobe.

In the summer of 2004, I considered an offer to coach the Los Angeles Lakers. It was the most seriously I'd ever looked at an NBA coaching position. And I knew that Kobe wanted me to take the job. Though I followed my heart and made the right decision to stay at Duke, it was another missed opportunity to coach the best player in the world.

In getting ready for my first summer as national coach in 2006, one of the things I was most excited about was that I would get that chance to coach Kobe. On the Fourth of July, my family got together for a celebration of the holiday. It was a fun day with my wife, my daughters, and their families. The American flags my wife had put up throughout the house had me feeling patriotic and eager to get started with the US team in just a few short weeks.

The celebration was interrupted by a phone call from Kobe. Happy to hear his voice, I took the call in another room. When I came back into the room where my family waited to hear what Kobe had to say, my mood had completely changed. "Kobe is not going to be able to play in the World Championships," I told them. "He's injured and he's going to need surgery." I had almost been Kobe's coach again, but still it was not to be.

Despite his inability to participate that summer, Kobe let me know of his intention to join the team the following year. Playing basketball for the United States was the one item missing from the story of his career and it had been a dream of his for a long time. And, just because he wasn't with us that summer didn't mean that we would stop cultivating our relationship. In fact, it became even more essential that we stay in touch with one another. As LeBron and I had done, Kobe and I communicated several times throughout the year. I kept one e-mail I received from him just before his Lakers team entered the playoffs. Incidentally, the subject line of that e-mail read, "Team."

In it, Kobe wrote, "I've been thinking about our US team and I can't wait to get started. I've been watching a great deal of European ball trying to learn their movements and tendencies. I think that our team should be filled with players who are willing to play for you. Guys who want to be coached so that you can do what you do best with no worries of communication between pro players and college coach." Here was Kobe, not only being a diligent student of the game, but also trying to set me at ease as a coach. As if I weren't already excited to have Kobe on my team, his e-mail's closing got me even more excited. It read, "Having players have a defensive DNA and desire goes without saying. I am ready to learn and excited to be coached by one of the best and looking forward to the thrill of a new challenge and the joy of a new kill."

A few months later, we were all to convene in Las Vegas for practice and participation the 2007 FIBA Americas Championship. Our staff came in two days before our players to meet and get organized. I was ready to get back to work with this team and to earn our qualification for the Olympics. And I was particularly gratified that I would *finally* be Kobe Bryant's coach.

When our coaches and USAB personnel gathered for our first dinner at SW Steakhouse in the Wynn Las Vegas hotel, Sean Ford informed me that Kobe was arriving in Vegas that night as well, two days before players were expected. I was surprised but remembered what LeBron had said about Kobe preparing the best of anyone. My enthusiasm to be Kobe's coach grew even more.

About halfway through the meal, Kobe walked into the private room where we were dining and we made a place for him next to me. After we had talked for a few minutes, Kobe asked me, "Coach, can you do me a favor?"

"And what's that?" I responded.

"I want you to let me guard the best player on every team we face. And I promise that I will destroy him." Here was possibly the greatest offensive player in the game asking me for the opportunity to play defense at the highest level. It was also his way of telling me that he was willing to adapt to help make us the best team we could become.

In our first team practice, without saying a word, Kobe made another statement. Throughout the entire practice, he did not take a shot. Not one. I called him over to talk. "You know that 'destroy' thing?" I asked.

He laughed. "Yeah, Coach. I promise you, I'll destroy them."

"Well you can destroy people on offense, too," I told him, "I just watched you score fifty or more points in ten different games this season. And last year, you had eighty-one points in a game. We're going to need you to score for us too."

"You know what I was trying to do," he responded. And I did know what he was trying to do. He was sending a message to his teammates and coaches that Kobe Bryant was a team player, that he was willing to adapt to a different role than he had with his Los Angeles Lakers. He knew as a leader that the example he would set by taking on this role would help immensely in our becoming a championship team.

That first day of practice was also time for us to distribute the uniforms we would wear for our Americas Championship games and to put them on for the first time as we posed together for our team photo. Nike did a beautiful job with the uniforms and used them to honor the 1960 Olympic team, who brought home the gold from Rome with such great players as Oscar Robertson and Jerry Lucas and was headed up by the legendary coach Pete Newell. On the inside of each uniform, the entire roster was listed as well as the scores of each game of their perfect 8-0 Olympic record. One of the stand-out names on that roster was Jerry West, who has said that his Olympic uniform is the only one he has ever worn that is on display in his home.

Kobe walked into the equipment room where the uniforms were laid out. He reverently stood in front of his number 10 jersey and stared down at the *U*, the *S*, and the *A*. Tears formed in his eyes as he said, "I've been waiting a long time to wear this uniform." People who have reached the level of success and celebrity that Kobe has are not often allowed opportunities to dream. But Kobe had dreamed about this moment, and his dream was coming true.

Where LeBron's leadership was loud, Kobe led mostly through the strength of example. But I wouldn't say he was quiet. He always had input for our staff during film sessions about how to best defend a particular player or an offensive play. And extending the message he sent by not shooting in our first practice, he rarely spoke about offense. Kobe invigorated our team defensively by relishing his role as a defensive stopper. Everyone knew what Kobe could do on the offensive end of the floor, but by always talking about defense Kobe taught our team that it was our most important collective focus.

While he can often seem stoic on the exterior, I found Kobe to be a very emotional player. What I mean by that is that his play is exponentially improved when he makes an emotional investment. Motivating Kobe was never difficult because he gives himself to you. There are no airs about him. He will be honest with you. Because we were always honest with one another from the beginning, our relationship came to be built on trust. So, when crucial moments arose for our team, we knew we could believe one another's words instantly.

Kobe was also the type of leader who would make the strong statements to our team, letting everyone share in his confidence. You have Kobe on your team and you just feel like you have a better chance of winning. Obviously, his talent makes you feel that, but so does his competitive nature. He is incredibly unique because he is that rare breed of person who lives for the crucial moment. People like Kobe find the ultimate high in the big game, the big moment, crunch time. When others would be shaking, he smiles. When others would be hesitating, he can't wait.

When my daughter Jamie asked Kobe about the development of our relationship from when I recruited him until now, Kobe told her, "I know I would have made the right decision going to Duke, because Coach K is who I thought he was." The feeling is mutual. In finally getting my opportunity to coach Kobe Bryant, I found that he is who I thought he was, too: one of the most talented basketball players in the history of the game and the unique kind of competitor that may come around only once in a leader's lifetime.

JASON KIDD MOMENTS

I wanted Jason Kidd to be on our team from the get-go. For various reasons, in our first summer together as a National Team it couldn't happen. After our loss to Greece, it became clear that our team needed to add some veteran players to our roster. Between the summers of 2006 and 2007, I kept calling Jerry Colangelo and telling him, "We need Jason Kidd." Jason had already won a gold medal in the 2000 Olympics and was undefeated in international play prior to joining our team. I was persistent. I wanted this guy on my team.

In 1993 my Duke team was pursuing its third straight National Championship and, in the second round of the NCAA tournament, we faced the University of California Bears, whose star player was Jason Kidd. He was brilliant, and Cal took us out of the tournament. In seeing what he did against our team, I witnessed first-hand what a special player he was. I was extremely happy the day my phone rang and it was Jerry on the other end saying, "Okay, Mike. We got your guy."

When it was time for our team to assemble on August 14, 2007, in Las Vegas for the Americas Championship, I had planned a team meeting for 8:00 p.m. in our team meeting room. But I had sent word to Jason, via Sean Ford, that I wanted to meet with him individually thirty minutes prior to our team meeting. We had made the decision to bring Jason in as a voice of experience. I knew that he was going to be a stabilizing force on this team, that he would bring wisdom and maturity to our group. Even though the players teased him and called him "Grandpa," at thirty-four years old he could still really play. As a player, Jason's court vision and his willingness to take a chance had always impressed me. He has a unique and explosive trinity of qualities as a point guard: talent, imagination, and courage.

At exactly 7:30 p.m., I heard a knock on my hotel room door. When I opened it, there was Jason Kidd carrying a notepad and pen and extending his hand to shake mine. Again, I was impressed. He was right on time. And he came prepared. As we shook hands, Jason said to me, "It's going to be an honor to play for you, Coach. And I'll do anything you want me to do."

"Well, I'm really looking forward to being your coach," I responded.

We sat down to talk face-to-face, and I told Jason what I had planned for that evening's team meeting. "I'm going to talk a little bit about what it means to be a champion," I told him. "And this summer, for us to be champions, I think we need to be three things. First, we need to be *unselfish*—with playing time and in making the extra pass. Second, we need to be *smart*—taking good shots and always being aware of time, score, and fouls. And third," I concluded, "we need to be *aggressive*—not just when we have the ball but in movement away from the ball. We need to hit the offensive boards and attack the passing lanes on defense." I told him all of this because I wanted his input. "What do you think?" I asked.

"I think that's great. I think all those things are important. But can I make one suggestion?" he asked.

"Certainly."

"I think we need to have an expectation of one another to be on time," he responded. "It shows respect." This was no trivial point. Jason wanted us to have the utmost respect for one another and for our team's mission.

"Would you be willing to say that at the meeting?" I asked him. "I'll say what I have to say and then ask if anyone has something to add. If you add your point then, it could really have an impact." Jason agreed.

When our team got together that night, I gave the speech I had planned. I told my team the three things that I thought it would take for us to become champions and then asked if anyone had something to add.

"Yeah, one more thing," Jason spoke up. "Champions are on

time." It meant more coming from him. Not only that, I wanted Jason's voice to be established on our team from the first meeting. This was the way that Jason would lead.

The next day, as we were going through drills in our first practice, I stood with Jason and picked his brain about roles on our team. When we spoke about his role, Jason reiterated, "Coach, you can bring me off the bench if you want to. Remember, I will do whatever you need me to do."

"You know what I need you to do?" I replied. "I need you to be instinctive. In fact, the next hundred things you do I want them to be instinctive. And I'll bet that ninety-nine of them turn out to be exactly what I would want you to do. You've played more games than I've coached. You know what needs to be done out there. I need you to lead us out on the court with your instincts. That's one of the things we were missing last summer."

"Not anymore," he responded.

Jason had reached out to me first by asking what I wanted from him and I had shown confidence in him and in his leadership by allowing him to be himself. *People are far more apt to develop a trusting relationship if they are allowed to be themselves.* From that moment on, the communication between our coaching staff and Jason Kidd was perfect.

When we qualified for the Olympics that summer it was apparent that Jason's flair for the game and his willingness to help everyone on the team had created the environment we needed to win. We were more mature, games were more fun, and all of us felt so much more confident as a result of his leadership. His impact was instantaneous.

In 2008, as we prepared for the Olympics at training camp, we had to devote some time to instill our offensive and defensive systems. As a result, some practices became more cerebral than physical. In these types of practices, there are more stop-actions. At times it is difficult to create a great flow. This was somewhat of a concern because of the limited number of practices we had. If your team is together for an entire seven-month season, you can have this type of practice without having to worry about conditioning every single day. But when your team has a small number of practices in a six-week season together, guys need to be running more.

During one of these cerebral practices, I called Jason over. "Some of our guys need to get some extra running in," I told him. "We need to be in great shape, and I think if the decision to do extra conditioning comes from the players and not the coaches, we will do it better."

"I'll take care of it," he responded. Before that practice was over, I noticed Jason Kidd on the sidelines with Dwight Howard running sprints up and down the court. If I had told the team, "Okay, I want you running sprints on the sidelines during downtime," it would have seemed like an order. Because it came from Jason, it was more like "Hey, let's do this, let's get better." Jason took the extra step to convey that message by running those sprints right along with Dwight.

And it was not only the logistical things that Jason was able to handle, he was also able to guide our team in the way we presented ourselves to the outside world. During our team's time together, we had the privilege of hearing our national anthem played many times as our team stood on the court before each game. Because our guys had great senses of context and perspective from the outset, they were always reverent as the song was played. But as we played more and more games together, I started to feel like reverence was not quite enough. We needed to be unified. Again, I went to Jason.

"When we hear our national anthem playing," I said to him, "I think we should all be doing the same thing."

Before I could even complete my request, Jason said, "Yeah Coach, we should all have our hands over our hearts. I'll take care of it." It was simple. It was easy. I just turned it over to Jason Kidd. I don't know what he said or did, and it really doesn't matter, but before our next game I witnessed a beautiful thing: all twelve guys listening to "The Star-Spangled Banner" with their hands over their hearts.

Jason's mind is his best talent. He sees things instinctively that others could study for years and never see. He also has a remarkable knowledge and respect for the game. I leaned on him tremendously for advice on how to get my message through to the team. Sometimes during timeouts, I would just let Jason do the talking.

I think contributions like the immeasurable ones Jason made to our team are often overlooked in business. Jason is still a young man in the grand scheme of things, but he is close to retirement age in our business. Much tends to fall into the hands of the newest up-and-comer. By being so quick to place everything in the hands of the young, I believe something is lost. I can't imagine our Olympic team without Jason.

Over his two summers with us, Jason was always comfortable and confident in his role on our team. He knew that he had something to offer that we didn't have without him. We, as a coaching staff, showed that we recognized the importance of this something by starting him in every game we played in the summer of 2008. Often, in both business and sport, people want to see the numbers; it is the numbers that tell us what someone has contributed. But in trying to understand one's value as a member of a team, there is no mathematical equation; not everything can be quantified. Simply put, there is no statistic that measures what Jason brought to our team.

The best way I can describe it is that he could feel the pulse of our team *all the time*. And, as a result, he knew what to say and when and how to say it. He never hesitated, because he knew he had the support of our staff. When I think back on our time together, I will hear his voice as much as any other. He guided us and we all listened. He was willing to give us everything he had, and we were willing to accept.

TAKE THE TIME

Take the time to cultivate leadership. Recognize that yours is not the only voice that your team wants or needs to hear, and be unselfish with your leadership. By allowing others to lead and by using their voices, you show that you are a stronger leader. Their voices can help you increase your team's attention-span window and can often convey a message that resonates in a way that could never have come from the leader.

Even though our US team didn't have captains, LeBron James, Kobe Bryant, and Jason Kidd really emerged as our leaders. They were all looked up to, and for different reasons. LeBron's leadership was extroverted, charismatic, exuberantly loud. Kobe's leadership was natural, he had a presence, he knew how to say the tough things, and he led by example in pressure situations. And Jason's leadership was quiet, stabilizing, veteran. We needed all of those things. Try to develop an understanding of the different leadership qualities individuals on your team may have. The best leadership your team can have is a combination of *your* strengths with *theirs*. You make up for one another's weaknesses.

Don't be intimidated by the talents of the other leaders among your team. Allow them to share your leadership. By cultivating your own relationship with your internal leaders, you can make a connection with them that ensures your group is unified in what you are doing and how you are doing it.

TIME TO LEARN
THE LANGUAGE

When bringing together a group of individuals from various backgrounds, you cannot automatically assume that you all speak the same language. For our team, the players came from all over the country and played on a number of different NBA teams, whereas Jim Boeheim and I came from the world of college basketball. You may form a business team made up of people from a range of departments or even different branches of your organization. From each of these locations comes a different way of communicating. It is essential to develop a common vocabulary and incorporate methods of getting your messages across to one another so that there is never any internal confusion.

Coming in as a college coach to lead a team of NBA players, I had to make some changes. One of the adjustments that I had to make was in learning how to communicate on the court. The players and coaches in the NBA can sometimes use different terminology in talking about the game. For example, in basketball there are several ways to defend the ball screen. One of those methods is something that Coach Boeheim and I would call a "trap." In the NBA, the coaches and players refer to the same play as a "blitz." For the most part, Coach Boeheim, my staff, and I made an effort to utilize the pro terminology, since that was what the players would be more likely to respond to instinctively. When your team enters a competitive environment, your communication must be such that you can react in an instant. There is no time for interpretation or misinterpretation. Because things happen with such rapidity, there is no time for discussion. We all have to speak the same language.

Your team's internal leadership can be a great help in bridging your internal language barrier. Leaders will try to speak the language of their teams as best they can, but when something is communicated player-to-player, it's in their vernacular. At times, we would convey messages to LeBron, Kobe, or Jason and rely on them to get those messages across to the rest of the team.

In addition to developing a common vocabulary among your team, you must prepare for competition by learning the language of the environment in which you will be operating. Watching an opera in Italian would be a moving experience for most people. You know it's beautiful, and even if you can't speak Italian, you can appreciate the fact that the music, words, and artists are expressing some very deep emotions. But your understanding of the opera and appreciation for its beauty cannot be complete unless you know the language. This was the approach we took in acclimating ourselves to the international game; we had to learn to speak the basketball language of the world.

For decades, our American coaches have traveled all over the world to share our knowledge of the game and teach its language to coaches and players. Those coaches and players have used that knowledge to develop their own game that is not exactly the same as the game we play in the NCAA or the NBA. The international game has its own rules and its own mind-set, its own language. In heading to the Olympics, theirs was the language we had to speak.

Moment: International Officials Address the Team— August 2, 2006—Las Vegas, Nevada

For the National Team, first and foremost, we had to come to an understanding of the literal differences between the rules of basketball in the United States and the rules that govern international play. I liken this to learning the fundamentals of a language—the words, the grammar rules. You cannot function until you have this fundamental understanding.

Just before we left the country in 2006, and on several other occasions over our three summers together, we had international officials talk to our team and explain the differences between our game and the international game in their own words. As a result, our players and staff were better able to internalize those differences and understand how they would affect the way we would play.

The ball is different. The international ball has twelve panels, whereas the ball used in the NBA and NCAA has eight panels. It also has two different colors. In the NCAA and NBA it's one color. In our game, because the ball is an extension of your hand, players develop a feel for the ball itself. And that feel affects so many things they do in the game. NBA players play over eighty games a year with the NBA ball; they would play only eight games in the Olympics with the international ball. They had to try to develop that same feel for a different ball in a much shorter period of time.

The court is different. The trapezoidal lane of the international game is wider at the baseline than the rectangular lane to which we were all accustomed. The change in lane shape alters a player's perspective on the court, especially the post players. Because of being farther away from the basket, a lot of low-post play is eliminated in international ball. Players also have to be more cognizant of three seconds in the lane offensively because the surface area of the lane is greater. Another difference in the structure of the court is that the three-point line in international play is three feet closer to the basket than in the NBA. Not only would this hone our focus on outside shooting, it would also make us more aware of the ease with which our opponents could put three points on the scoreboard.

The length of the game is different. The international game is forty minutes long, four ten-minute quarters. The players on our team were used to playing four twelve-minute quarters. Not only that, but as the star players on their respective teams they were used to pacing themselves in order to play the majority of those forty-eight minutes. On our team, no one player had to put in that amount of time. There were fresh and very able legs waiting on the bench. From the start, we had a mantra for our team of "No pacing. Play every play." It is hard to believe that because there are eight fewer minutes to play, you have around 30 fewer possessions in the international game. But it's true, and it means that every single play becomes that much more important.

The foul situation is different. When playing the international game, we had to have an awareness of our team fouls. Once a team has committed its fifth foul in any given quarter, the opposing team is awarded two free-throw opportunities. We had to learn the international language by understanding the implications of the rule, and make "Remember team fouls" a part of our internal vocabulary. And we learned it effectively. During our eight games in the Olympics we shot 219 free throws to our opponents' 156.

But maybe *the biggest difference between international basketball and American basketball is the level of physical play.* This is not a rule, per se. It is not a part of the international basketball grammar. But really grasping a new language it not just about understanding its fundamentals. It is about proving ultimate respect for a different way of doing things by learning the cultural nuances. These nuances may be even more important than the language itself.

One of those nuances that we had to understand was that international basketball is very physical. Officials will allow the defense to have more contact when guarding the ball. You can do more to restrict the movements of offensive players without a foul being called. Not only did we have to prepare ourselves for the physical wear and tear due to this contact, we had to prepare ourselves mentally that this was not personal; it was simply how they play. We couldn't complain to officials, always remaining aware of the faces that we show during competition. Those faces needed to reflect strength. To complain to an official, even with just a facial expression or gesture, would irritate them and distract us from what we should be doing on the court. Even more, it would show the competition that we didn't understand their game, that we couldn't speak their language. If they saw that, they would know that their game was getting to us and they would feel that we were fighting the game, not fighting them. It would be a boost to our opponents.

Another change in mind-set had to do with the format of international tournaments. The concept of elimination games is entirely different in FIBA play. In the NBA Playoffs our guys had grown accustomed to playing a series of up to seven games leading to one team's elimination. In the medal round of the Olympics, single elimination forces you to win *this* game, not to focus on an accumulation of wins over several games. The stakes are higher on a game-to-game basis. One and done.

Pool play also created a unique challenge. A team could lose one, two, even three games in Olympic pool play and still have a chance to win the gold medal. Because of this, many international teams use pool play games strategically. They may throw some offenses and defenses at you that they would not use in the medal rounds. They may experiment with lineups. In effect, it is okay with them to lose a battle as long as they win the war. We approached every game like it was a war, because to lose even one game would be a blemish on our mission. I believe that if we had lost a game, even if it had been in pool play or one of our exhibitions, people would have viewed our effort as a partial failure.

Using the tell-show-do approach to teaching, we had asked the officials to *tell* the players of the differences in the game. Next, we asked them to *show* us some examples on tape. And then, for many of our practices over our three years together, we asked international referees to officiate our scrimmages, giving the players the opportunity to incorporate what they had learned into what they actually *do*. When calls were made, we asked the officials to stop play and explain the call in the context of the international game. This way, our players and staff could understand how the rules were interpreted in action, not merely in theory.

In any business, one has to recognize that the rules governing your industry on a global stage may be different than those that govern the way we operate within the United States. Our country's dominance for many years in many areas has given us an arrogance that could render us ill-prepared to engage internationally. Basketball is no exception. We had to create a culture to compete with those who were doing well in our market. And today, in the ever-expanding global market of basketball, the United States is just one of many outstanding competitors.

Moment: Scrimmaging the US Select Team— July 21, 2008—Las Vegas, Nevada

In most businesses, one of the best ways to ingrain an understanding of the competition's language is to simulate. For us, this meant bringing in NBA players who were not on our twelve-man Olympic roster to replicate the offenses, defenses, and styles of play of the competition we would face in China. This was what the very talented USA Basketball Select Team did for us in both 2007 and 2008 and what my great friend P.J. Carlesimo and Jay Triano of the Toronto Raptors gave us in volunteering to coach the Select players. The USA Basketball Select Team was a group of ten young NBA players in 2007 and fourteen in 2008 who traveled to Las Vegas to train and practice the style of our international opponents in order to drill or scrimmage against the Senior National Team. Like the thirty-three players in our National Team pool, these young men made a commitment of both their time and talent in pursuit of the goal that belonged to all of us.

P.J. and I were on the coaching staff of the US team that competed in the 1990 World Championships in Argentina, the last US team to feature college players on the World Championship and Olympic level. P.J. and I also shared an amazing experience as two of the assistant coaches for the first US team made up of professional players with the Dream Team in 1992. In addition, P.J. had coached in college, the NBA, and internationally, and he had given many basketball clinics all over the world. He possessed extensive knowledge, and it was easy to work with him because of the relationship that we shared. While he was in Las Vegas with us, I asked him to sit in on all our staff and team meetings so that we could gain the most from what he had to offer while developing our team. Going up against players like Andre Igoudala, Kevin Durant, Al Jefferson, and JJ Redick, coached by one of the best in P.J., made us better prepared for the talented opposition we would face in Olympic play.

In 2008, the Select Team arrived at training camp a day early to learn the offenses and defenses that some of the international teams would utilize. The next morning, before heading to practice where we would scrimmage the Select Team for the first time that summer, we asked Jay Triano to speak to the team. Jay was also a real asset for us in learning the language of international basketball, having been both a player and head coach for the Canadian National Team. Not only that, Jay brought with him knowledge of the professional game from his position as an assistant coach for the Toronto Raptors, where he is now head coach. With their backgrounds, he and P.J. both understood the game from which our players were coming and the direction we needed to go to compete on the world's stage. They knew the language of both.

Jay reminded us of three things to think about when facing international competition. The first was the physicality. "The international teams are known for their physical play," Jay explained, "and the international referees are not as likely to call those fouls as NBA officials. The other teams will do anything they can to get under your skin and get you thinking about something other than what your job is."

Second, he emphasized the fact that there are fewer possessions in international games. "Not only that," he said, "but those other teams will try to slow the game down even more. They want you guys to play selfishly on offense." It was assumed that our NBA players would revert to their individual instincts when tested. In preparing for international play, in learning the language of their game, we had to be prepared for this type of challenge.

The third thing he mentioned was that international teams would pack in their defenses, meaning that they would crowd the lane, hoping to force us to take jump shots. They knew our athletes could drive the ball and score close to the basket, so they would gamble on our being unable to shoot from the outside. This was the way the Select Team, under P.J. and Jay, trained to compete against us. And, with these reminders from Jay, we headed to the gym.

For the first half of practice, while we ran drills and sets, P.J. and Jay would run their own practice in an adjacent gym. Then, we would bring the Select Team in to join us and run drills or scrimmage against them. During this time, the international officials would call the drills and scrimmages to keep us aware of the new language we were learning.

We scrimmaged against the Select Team several times for short periods, usually ten minutes. We won most of those scrimmages, but we also lost a few. One of the wins that stands out in my memory came down to a last-second shot. LeBron had sprained his ankle early in the practice but was continuing to encourage his US teammates from the sideline. It was Kobe who took that last-second shot, a three-pointer. Before the ball even left Kobe's hands, LeBron said from the sideline, "Game time." And he was right. Nothing but net.

It was exciting to have all of those guys on the court together, the stars of today along with those of tomorrow. Sean Ford described it by saying, "It was a good sight for USA Basketball, at the end of a workout to see 26 NBA players, all with USA on their uniforms." It's the way that the national program should be: a collective effort on the part of our basketball community to ensure that we put our best foot forward in international competition.

Moment: Tony Ronzone Addresses the Team—July 24, 2008—Las Vegas, Nevada

One of several changes we made to our team and staff following our loss in the 2006 World Championships was to bring in Tony Ronzone as director of international player personnel. Tony's day job is director of basketball operations for the Detroit Pistons, where he directs all the franchise's international scouting. I always wanted to hear Tony's input because he is one of the most well-traveled people I know. He certainly has unsurpassed knowledge of international basketball, having played professionally in a number of different countries and coached for several international teams, including the Chinese National Team in 2001. Tony traveled more than any of us over his two years on our staff; prior to the Olympics, he followed the international teams we would face to scout them. He is the best at what he does as an international scout because he really loves international basketball. His total respect for international players helped us learn to respect that game even more.

Another quality that makes Tony good at his job is that he has great relationships with some of the key personnel in international ball and knows how they think. On the day we asked him to address our team before we left for China, he had an important message for us. "You have to know that the international players watch you guys very closely. They learned the game from you but they are very educated now, and they believe that USA Basketball has lost the love," he told our guys. "They don't believe that what we're doing now is real. They think that in the heat of battle, we are going to revert to being individuals and that we are not going to play team basketball." He ended with his most important message: "We can change that perception."

I think the way that Tony talked about the globalization of basketball can be applied to any business going global. "We have a great product," he said, "but it has to be a winner on and off the court." In other words, it wasn't just about finding success again in our normal business operations; it wasn't just about winning basketball games. It was about being respectful of the now-international culture of the game. People like Tony are vital to any business looking to globalize. You must have someone with the right background who can take the time to study the international environment thoroughly and share those things with your team. In our particular case, part of understanding the international language was recognizing the way in which we were viewed by our competition. They did not yet believe that we believed. They did not think we could become brothers. They thought we would disintegrate under pressure. Our mission became more than winning the gold—it became winning the gold in a manner that would regain international respect.

TAKE THE TIME

Take the time to learn the language. First, make certain that your team is speaking the same internal language. Remember that your team is likely comprised of individuals from different backgrounds who talk about things in different ways. As a part of the installation of your team's system of communication, make sure that you develop a common vocabulary. When doing so, it helps to have cultivated your relationships with leaders on your team who can always communicate your team's message to the group in their vernacular.

Once you are comfortable that your team is speaking the same internal language, take the time to learn the language of the competition, both the fundamentals and the subtleties of the environment in which you will be operating. Seek advice from people who know that language better than you; ask them to teach you and to help you find ways to simulate so that you can internalize that new language at a higher level.

When you come to understand that language, whether literal or figurative, you earn respect for having prepared in the right way. People will realize that you do not presumptuously believe that everyone is going to learn your language. In the globalized world of both business and sport, it is no longer about people striving to do things like we do them in the United States. Instead, we have become one of many competitors. We still have a great product—it's just a matter of learning enough about our competitive environment to present that product in a manner that conveys ultimate respect for all the languages in your particular business world.

TIME TO ADAPT INTERNALLY

In the formation of teams, every single person must adapt. And for those who have met with much individual success, adaptability can be a challenge. To use a business analogy, the formation of our Olympic team was more like the coming together of a corporate conglomerate than the establishment of a small company. Each individual player on our team was a successful company in his own right, appearing in numerous advertisements, and earning millions of dollars; each was supported by a large fan base and his own multiperson support staff.

At our first meeting in the summer of 2006, Jerry Colangelo told our team, "Check your egos at the door." Jerry was referring to a crucial concept of team building: the sacrifice of the individual ego and the establishment of a stronger, joint ego. International teams had been doing this for years. Kobe Bryant explained it best when he pointed out that LA Laker teammate Pau Gasol was certainly a force in the NBA but, when playing for his native Spain, "he was Superman." Gasol was elevated to the best version of himself when competing for his country. In international programs, becoming a part of a country's Senior National Team is a progression, something that you work for from childhood. That, of course, is not the way it has been in the United States. This was an area in which the US team had fallen disastrously behind.

To ensure that the collective identity of the team is a combination of everyone's best, leaders must recognize that everyone brings their own good stuff to the table. It may be different from your stuff, but at the same time, it may be much better. You cannot simply ask your team to just adapt to you. As a leader, it is part of your responsibility to adapt as well. If everyone simply adjusts to the style of the leader, you are not getting the most of what everyone has to offer. *Instead, a leader needs to be a part of a mutual adaptation that forms a combination of the best of everyone.* That is the type of environment that encourages us all to become Superman.

Moment: Lunch with Coach D'Antoni— April 18, 2006—Phoenix, Arizona

As soon as Jerry and I knew the makeup of our coaching staff, I wanted to learn much more about Mike D'Antoni and Nate McMillan. Jim Boeheim and I had been friends and colleagues for over thirty years, so I was already very familiar with both his personality and coaching style. He was also very familiar with mine. I wanted his knowledge and the trust that we had built over those thirty years with me every step of the way. Of course, I recognized the fact that all three coaches were among the best coaches in the game at any level. But I also recognized that for us to be as good as we could be, they all had to be engaged. As a staff, we had to adapt to each other as opposed to submitting to the style of any one of us.

Part of this, though, was making sure that everyone was comfortable with their role. Much of this can be accomplished by making clear your own willingness to make changes. Before the National Team experience, I had never met Coach D'Antoni, so we set up a time to have lunch. I already knew that as a player, he had been the Michael Jordan of Italy. After retiring from playing, he also became one of the top coaches in Europe. So he brought with him a great knowledge of both the NBA game and the international game. I was excited to find out at that lunch just how much he would offer.

Almost immediately when I met Mike, I wanted to get the obvious out of the way. I asked him directly, "Are you okay with my being a college coach and leading this team?"

"Of course," he responded, with a laugh. You could tell right away what I learned to feel even more over time: Mike D'Antoni is a great guy, a great coach, and a great friend. "Don't worry, Coach," he told me, "I don't feel any of that stuff."

He called me "Coach." In fact, he and Nate McMillan called me "Coach" throughout the three summers we worked together. Jim Boeheim and I have a few years on those guys so it may have been a function of age. As a result, though, they found a simple way to set me at ease on a daily basis that they were comfortable with my being the head coach.

But being a leader means ensuring that everyone else is comfortable, too, and that your team gets the most out of your leadership by getting something from everyone. "Okay," I said to Mike, "just remember that we are all head coaches in our day jobs and we should act like co–head coaches here. You should speak up and say what you want to say. And I will especially lean on you for offense."

This was *our* team, not mine. So from the start, we all three recognized what each other had accomplished. D'Antoni knew the NBA players and understood what they each did best. He was able to incorporate their abilities into an offense that I liked so much that I have begun to use some of it with my Duke team. I had coached against Nate McMillan when he played at North Carolina State in the 1980s. He brought amazing defensive credentials with him from his time in college and as a two-time NBA All-Defensive Team player during his twelve-year playing career with the Seattle SuperSonics. Nate was able to help me teach the players the kind of defense that I wanted to play with our team because—while the defense itself was more like college in terms of guarding passing lanes and playing help-side—we were teaching it to players on his level. He facilitated that learning. And Jim Boeheim was not only a great friend of mine, he was a Hall-of-Famer, a National Championship coach in 2003, and a master of zone defense and offense. He was responsible for putting in our zone, which was named "Orange" after his Syracuse team. The three men who served as assistant coaches on this Olympic team were invaluable.

Moment: Nick Arison Unloads Boxes—
July 17, 2006—Las Vegas, Nevada

Nick Arison was a manager for my Duke Basketball teams during his four years as an undergraduate. He was always fully committed and was a uniquely hard worker. After graduating, Nick joined the staff of the Miami Heat, which is owned by his father, Micky Arison. As he had always done, Nick worked his way up the organizational ladder to a prime position in the organization's upper management. On September 29, 2008, Nick was named the Miami Heat's vice president of basketball operations.

When I needed to bring together support staff for the National Team, Nick was at the top of my list. He had worked with USA Basketball once before in the 2004 Athens Olympics and was a close friend of myself and my family. When asked to come back and again distribute towels, mix Gatorade, help run drills, and manage the team's gear, Nick eagerly accepted. Under the leadership of USAB Competitive Programs Manager Ellis Dawson, Nick became a big part of our USAB support staff. When it comes to competition, a leader wants every person on their team to feel inspired. Ellis and Nick would never take the court for us, but their contributions were incredibly important. I wanted them to feel competitive about their jobs. And they did have that feeling.

Example: in 2008, they were responsible for ensuring the safe arrival of 170 pieces of luggage that went from Las Vegas to Beijing and contained our players' personal items, uniforms, and expensive video equipment. The job was nothing to take lightly, either in difficulty or importance. On the way to Macau, we had to take two airplanes, three buses, and a ferry to reach our destination, not to mention having to go through customs. After five days in Macau, we traveled to Shanghai by plane to spend four days there before finally flying to Beijing. Not one piece of luggage was lost and Ellis and Nick's work never slowed us down.

In the summer of 2006, when my wife, Mickie, and I arrived in Las Vegas for the team's very first training camp, Nick's team, the Miami Heat, had just won an NBA Championship. Mickie went to the training room at the Wynn hotel where the USAB staff had begun assembling and saw Nick moving boxes full of USAB gear and sweating profusely. "Well, Nick," she said to him, "I think the last time I saw you, you were doing this exact same thing," referring to his time as a Duke manager.

"Probably," he replied, "but this time I'm doing it with an NBA Championship ring on my finger."

Nick is a terrific example of finding meaning in becoming a part of something bigger than you. He is simply a team guy, and daily he set a great example for our team. Here was maybe the next owner of the Miami Heat willing to perform the managerial duties that defined his role. In sacrificing his individual ego, in being willing to adapt and give everything he has for a team cause, Nick has become a part of some amazingly successful teams: a National Championship team in 2001 at Duke, an NBA Championship team in 2006 with Miami, and now an Olympic gold-medal team in 2008 with USA Basketball. I know that Nick would tell you that in team building, the sacrifice is well worth the reward.

Moment: Nike Olympic Uniform Presentation— June 27, 2008—Las Vegas, Nevada

Before going to our first 2008 practice, where we would don our Olympic uniforms for the first time for a team photo, Ryan

Aanderud, creative design director for Nike Basketball, gave a PowerPoint presentation to our team. He introduced the concept behind the uniforms and explained the significance of the creative detail that was in the design. To me, those uniforms so effectively conveyed the idea of sacrificing the individual ego for the much stronger collective one. And for us, that collective ego would be fed by the fact that we were representing the United States. Before that presentation, I had no idea how complex the uniform design process had been. I was unprepared for the beauty and meaning behind it all.

Ryan began his presentation by showing photographs of iconic American places and people: the Golden Gate Bridge, the Chicago skyline, the Hollywood sign, Rosa Parks, Abraham Lincoln, Rosie the Riveter, Jackie Robinson. Then he showed us images of icons within our own sport: Jerry West, Michael Jordan, Magic Johnson. The point of it all was: who are we representing? Finally, up on the screen a map of the United States appeared with the number 303,146,284 inside. This was who we were representing: the population of our country, over 300 million people from many different backgrounds.

The artist then told us that the design for the uniform and for much of the Nike USA Basketball merchandise would be centered around a "tattoo" he created entitled "We The People." The tattoo illustrated both the cultural diversity and the unity of the United States. Elements of many cultures were woven into the design: African symbols of strength and unity, Native American eagles, Asian American dragons, a Latin American bleeding heart, and Anglo and European American influences as well as allusions to our Founding Fathers and the US Constitution. The centerpiece of the tattoo was a torch, which brought to mind both the Statue of Liberty and the Olympic flame, both key icons to our team culture. The various cultural elements all came together at that torch to symbolize a nation unified in support of its Olympic teams. As the designer himself put it, "The overall look of the piece was created to have a unifying effect, only to hint at the legitimate styles and nuances that each culture might be known for. It is about how all these elements are just that, elements. Elements that create one overall force through diversity and unity at the same time. An overall statement is being made here that while we are all diverse culturally, as Americans we come together and create our own way of living, our own style, our own team . . . while staying true to ourselves."

I loved hearing his passion for the art he had created. But my favorite part of our uniforms was something more obvious to the casual observer: the way the individual names of the players appeared so subtly on the backs of the uniforms. On our white uniforms, the last names appeared in white, outlined in a faint grey, barely noticeable. On the blue uniforms, the names were in a blue identical to the color of the uniform itself, outlined in white, again inconspicuous. It would take more than a glance to read the player names. Conversely, the name on the front of the jersey—"USA"—popped from the background of both the white and the blue uniforms in a vibrant red. You couldn't miss it. What better way to send the message that we were playing for the name on the front of the jersey and not the name on the back than to have one stand out so much more vividly than the other? It was a way of expressing our collective identity over our individual identities every moment we were on the court together.

Moment: Adjusting to Our Surroundings— August 10, 2008—Beijing, China

In addition to adapting to one another, we had to adapt to our surroundings and be flexible. Typically before one of our games, the coach who had conducted the scouting report would write out the opponent's personnel on the locker-room whiteboard. When we went into our Wukesong Arena locker room for the first time before our game against China, we saw that the board provided would be too small to accommodate the scouting report. In fact, it was not merely too small, it was ridiculously small—the size of whiteboards that you would find hanging on dorm-room doors. Always flexible, our staff came up with a solution. They found a cardboard trash can, unfolded it, hung it on the wall, and wrote on it our scouting report against China. Sean Ford took a great photograph of it as a reminder of the need to be adaptable. It makes me laugh to look at that picture and envision players like LeBron James, Kobe Bryant, and Dwight Howard studying the scouting report written with a Sharpie on a cardboard trash can. But just like people writing songs on diner napkins or business ideas on matchbook covers, it got the job done.

The locker-room setup was less than ideal in other ways as well. Instead of the traditional single large room where an entire team can gather, our Olympic locker room was divided into two small rooms joined by a smaller hallway. There was no way an entire team could fit in either one of those rooms, so it was nearly impossible to address the team as a whole. This created another ridiculous picture: all of these supersized men crowded in one little room, some of the staff who were unable to fit peering in from their spot huddled in the hallway. At the front of the room, next to our trash-can scouting report, there was room for only one coach to speak to the team at a time. I stood sideways next to Mike D'Antoni while he went over the personnel, then we shuffled around to switch positions so that I could speak to the team while Mike stood sideways next to me. It was like being in Times Square on New Year's Eve. Really, it was comical. But again, we made it work.

Partially because of the awkward locker-room setup, we created space specifically for our team at the Intercontinental. In our "home" environment at the hotel, we established a team room on the sixth floor that became an extension of our locker room. Only team and staff were allowed in that room. While we would typically eat our meals together with our families in the larger fifth-floor meal room, we used the team room to eat our pregame meals. It helped us immensely in getting into game mode. Since we did not actually change into uniforms at the arena, we came dressed in our uniforms to pregame meals. Teams need both time and space to come together before a game, and by creating this space for them away from everything, we gave them what they needed to get focused. From that room, we went directly to the team bus already in a team frame of mind. By the time we arrived at the arena, we had game focus.

Moment: Conversation with Chris Paul and Deron Williams—August 13, 2008—Beijing, China

A basketball team should check their egos at the door but should also pick them back up on their way onto the court. What I mean is, there is a delicate balance when it comes to asking people to adapt. You never want an individual to be so deferential to the team concept that they lose the part of their individual ego that makes them great. On our team we wanted to find the right mix of sacrifice and self-assurance that would allow each one of our guys to become Superman.

At our practice the day before we would face Greece in pool play, I pulled Chris Paul and Deron Williams aside to talk to them about ego. But it was not the kind of ego talk that many people would guess I had with these NBA All-Stars. I *never* had to have a talk with any player about being too egotistical. I actually had to ask Chris and Deron to allow their egos to show through more in order to make our team as good as it could be. Chris and Deron, like the rest of our National Team, completely subscribed to the concept of adapting to become a part of something bigger than them. They had been deferential to the veteran point guard, Jason Kidd, and had learned a lot from him. But it was time for them to let more of their own egos come back into play.

"In the rest of our games," I told those two guys, "I don't want you to just take USA Basketball shots. I want you to take New Orleans Hornets shots, Chris. And, Deron, I want you to take Utah Jazz shots." In other words, I wanted them to remember who they were: NBA All-Star players, franchise players on their individual teams. I wanted them to find the perfect place where the individual ego and the collective team ego meet to bring out the very best in an individual. They listened, and for the remaining games of the Olympics those Hornets and Jazz shots in USA uniforms helped us win gold.

TAKE THE TIME

Take the time to adapt internally. Remember that everyone on a team must adapt, including the leader, so that your team benefits from the best of each member. Your team will not be the best that it can be if everyone adapts to a single individual. *When leaders make clear their willingness to change, it establishes an environment in which everyone can be comfortable adapting.* And that collective identity you form, comprised of something great from everyone, elevates all of you in competition.

Remember that the sacrifice is worth the reward because teams can accomplish things that no one individual could ever accomplish alone. In the process, you want everyone in your organization to feel competitive and as if they have contributed something to the collective team ego, because they have.

A team should check their individual egos at the door, but only to a certain extent. Adapting internally to become a part of a team does not mean completely giving up your ego. It means developing a new team ego that is bigger than all of your individual egos combined. But it is also important to be confident enough to be yourself. Encourage the members of your team to make the best of both egos.

TIME TO PRACTICE

In planning for a team's progress, the leader has to examine how much time the team actually has to train before facing its challenge. How many meetings will our marketing team have before the big event? How many workshops can we go through before our big presentation? How many days can we practice before the big game? Before a company releases a product, there are many "practice" stages: research and development, product trials, limited releases. You would never send a product into the market before it's ready. It is the same way with sports teams.

If you have planned properly, your team should spend much more time in practice than in games. Practice is the grunt work, the everyday routine. Undoubtedly, it is not as exciting as a game. But it is where you develop habits. The way you practice will determine the way that you play.

I do believe that strong relationships are the foundation for great teams and that team bonding is essential. But there is also a time in which it is important to create competition among the members of your team. Just as a team gets better as a whole in the face of competition, players improve individually when internal competition is created during practice. Your players are given the opportunity to evolve into better individual contributors when there is something at stake. In basketball, this often means dividing your team into groups wearing two different colored jerseys, one of which is always white, the color of the home uniform in basketball. In practice, those white jerseys indicate the current starters or the top six players. People will compete for the chance to wear them. As a result, the members of your team will make each other better.

I also used National Team practices as an opportunity to get messages across to individual players. My goal was to seek out at least three guys at each practice and try to have personal interaction with them. Sometimes I had an agenda, a particular message that I needed to get across; other times I just wanted to touch them and let them know that they were on the minds of the coaching staff and that they were important to the team. A leader wants all members of a team to feel included and invested all the time.

For every practice in my career as a head coach—from my five years at Army, to my nearly thirty years at Duke, to my three summers as National Coach—I have spent time planning and writing out each day's practice plan by hand. While of course there is some overlap in the things we do in practice from day to day and from year to year, every practice plan is different. The cabinets in my office at Duke are lined with notebooks filled with the practice plans for every team that I have coached. I will refer back to those notebooks in preparation for each season. They help me recall what teaching sequence I may have used before, what drills I may have used in past seasons, and how basketball terminology has changed over the years. Now I also refer back to National Team practice plans; trying to determine what things we worked on in USAB practices may be a benefit to my Duke team.

At the conclusion of every team practice, I spend time thinking about what we have just done and what we need to accomplish in the next twenty-four hours. And part of what is included in my practice plan is what I will say to the team in our pre-practice meeting. That meeting is one of the times in which our relationships are cemented and lines of communication are established. As such, practice does not start in the gym; it starts at that meeting.

I also try to think about which players I may want to single out for personal interaction, whether it be on the bus, while the players are getting taped and lacing up their shoes, during practice itself, or while they are working on individual shooting at the end. I ask myself what players may need me to reach out to them on that particular day and from what players I need to gain insights.

The practice plan that I write up for each session with my teams serves as a guide. I use it to take me through the time that I have with my players on that day. But once practice time begins, I run motion offense with my plan. "Motion offense" refers to a type of offense that calls for flexibility and decision making. There are not set plays. Instead players make reads and determine what they will do based on what they see. Using the concepts that govern motion offense, I can make changes as I deem necessary. If something is not going well, we make an adjustment. If something originally planned no longer seems to fit, we eliminate it. Having a guide does not mean we cannot be flexible. We can watch what is going on and say we need more contact or there is too much contact. We can watch and decide that it's going too slowly and we need to substitute what we had planned with a competitive shooting drill. The practice plan is a living thing; it is fluid and ever-changing. But writing out the plan beforehand is a step I always take. I can't ask my players to be prepared to improve and to pursue our goal if I am not prepared.

I also try to coordinate with my assistant coaches to know the practice plan ahead of time. With the National Team, I always distributed the plan in our coaching staff meeting prior to the players' joining us for the team meeting. This gave us the time to discuss the plan and to get on the same page. It gave them the opportunity to ask for clarification on things or to suggest any changes they thought we might need to make based on their assessment of the previous practice. Distributing the practice plan is not like giving out orders. It is a framework for how the practice will go. It gave all the coaches the opportunity to individualize the portions of practice that they would lead in addition to contributing ideas for the run of practice as a whole.

I love practice. It is when a coach exercises the most control over the improvement of his or her team. In a game, someone else is trying to stop you from playing your best. But when it is just you, your team, and the game of basketball, there is no one stopping you from having a good practice—no competitor, no opposing crowd. This means that *you* can't stop you from having a good practice by being ill-prepared, unenthusiastic, or unwilling to adjust.

Moment: Finding Our Competitive Edge— May 7, 2006—Phoenix, Arizona

Once you have taken the time to learn the language of your particular endeavor, you can better understand the work that must be done. In learning the language, your team has become familiar with those things that the competition does well, those things on which you must improve. Speaking the language of the competition is one thing that you train for during practice.

But practice is also about developing your strengths. Having already analyzed our weaknesses and what the competition does better, we must also take time to determine where we find our competitive advantage. What are the things that your team can do better than the opposition? The answer comes from investigating the competition in addition to analyzing your own talent and resources. The way you practice, then, is determined both by the language of your competitive environment and what you find to be your own competitive edge.

A discussion of what our competitive advantage might be was a topic of conversation the day after our first staff gathering at Bianco's restaurant in Phoenix. After enjoying each other's company the previous evening at dinner, it was time to get down to business. We all knew what we wanted to accomplish, and now we had to begin discussing how we were going to do it. It was necessary that the meeting include a lot of logistical conversation: when we would come together to train, where we would practice, how we would travel, what we would wear, how we would communicate information to the team—all important decisions in figuring out how to achieve our goal. We devoted our morning session to these logistics.

When we reconvened in the afternoon, it was time to talk basketball. In discussing the group of players we would have and the competition we would face, all the coaches agreed that our team would find its competitive advantage on the defensive end of the floor. While international teams knew each other, knew their coaches, and understood their systems as second nature, it just didn't seem to be a part of the international basketball psyche to shut people down defensively. But our athleticism lent itself to hard, aggressive team defense. We could play to exhaustion because of our depth, we could switch more because of our versatility, and we could incorporate a variety of lineups that would ensure other teams could not get comfortable in an offensive flow. We could unite our strengths into a defense that could put a wrench in the gears of their offenses.

Based on this determination of our competitive edge, I constantly told our team, "We are not going to let them *run* plays. We want to force them to *make* plays." If we could disrupt their system, we could reduce them to a group of individuals on the court as opposed to a team. It was a matter of using our competitive edge to strip them of theirs.

On our team, there were two things that we talked about every single day: the gold medal and defense, our goal and our competitive edge. Those are two pretty important things for your team to always have on their mind. Once you have identified your competitive edge, your team talk begins to center around that aspect of your game. It becomes your mantra. And that mantra unites you even further. Deron Williams said, "I think our defense is always key for us. Defense is always our bread and butter, always our starting point, because if we're playing good D, we're going to get out in transition; we're going to run because we're creating turnovers and forcing miscues." If we could play defense in this way, we knew our opponents would be forced to adapt on the offensive end.

What made our competitive advantage especially difficult for the teams we faced was the fact that our intensity and athleticism could not be simulated. In our practices, we could have a group run international offensive sets. But they would have a difficult time preparing for the defense that they would face in a game against our team.

By the time we were ready to compete in the 2008 Olympic Games, we had become very proficient in capitalizing on our competitive advantage. Our opponents found themselves unable to make passes they had made their whole careers because players like Dwyane Wade and LeBron James were covering the passing lanes, and others like Deron Williams and Chris Paul were playing aggressive on-the-ball defense. Our team and the 1992 Dream Team are the only American teams in Olympic history with three players averaging more than two steals. Indeed, the statistical story from the Olympics illustrates how sharpening our competitive edge through practice led to our success. Leading the Olympic field in steals, blocks, two-point defensive percentage, three-point defensive percentage, forced turnovers, and points-off turnovers, we were able to disrupt the continuity of our opponents' carefully timed offenses.

Our defense had come a long way in the three years we spent as a National Team. Of the twenty-four teams that had participated in the 2006 World Championship Games, our team had placed sixteenth in defending against our opponents' two-point shooting and thirteenth in defending against the three. In the 2008 Olympics we were first in both categories, allowing our opponents to convert on only 46 percent of their two-point attempts and 30 percent from beyond the three-point arc. We also forced 19.3 turn-overs a game, more than five greater than any other team in the Olympics. As a result, we also shot the highest percentage from the floor because of frequent opportunities at fast-break points off those turnovers. As you always hope for in basketball, our defense produced offense.

Moment: First Olympic Training Camp Practice— July 21, 2008—Las Vegas, Nevada

Once our team gathered for our final training camp in late July, we would be together for the duration, culminating in the gold-medal game on August 24, 2008. Mini-camp and our motivational trip to New York City had served to prepare our minds for our mission and to unite us with a common emotion. This training camp would be about the body, doing the physical things that we needed to do to prepare us for competition.

We started off every practice by stretching, getting our guys physically ready for the rigors of a practice session. This stretching was led by one of our two athletic trainers, Casey Smith, who is the head trainer for the Dallas Mavericks. Our other trainer was Keith Jones, the Houston Rockets' head trainer. Both Keith and Casey had extensive experience in taking care of US teams in in-ternational competition. The two of them were always in tune with what was going on with our players and were an enormous asset in relaying that information to me. Our trainers would sit in the seat in front of me on the bus on the way to practice and games and, besides giving me updates on the team's physical status, they would let me know the team's mood. A trainer's job is to make a player feel good, so trainers listen with a sympathetic ear. Often the players will open up to a trainer more than they would to a coach. I would ask Keith and Casey, "Are we ready?" and they'd say, "The guys are really ready" or "The guys are running low on energy today." Both of them made a commitment to being a part of the team for all three summers despite the fact that their jobs with Dallas and Houston required as much of a time commitment from them as any of our players. As a result of their commitment, our players stayed healthy and happy throughout our gold-medal pursuit.

Casey had the expertise to lead a stretching session that would be of the most benefit in preparing our athletes for practice and preventing injury. When gathered in a big circle on the court to stretch, our team found this was also a great time for the guys on the team to communicate. They became attuned to each other's voices, and that got their minds prepared to play on the court together. Often these were the times in which LeBron was at his funniest. Even though the players were talking and laughing, they were stretching their bodies—and minds—before we began our drills.

In between plays at that first practice, I noticed Kobe take Carmelo by the arm and point something out to him about our defense. I took the time to stop practice and tell the team that I loved when our players coached one another. "This is exactly what we need on the court," I said to them. "We need to constantly be talking and communicating."

A leader can try his or her very best but will never know every single thing that is taking place in practice. Practice, then, is another time in which empowering members of your staff and the players themselves pays off. Carmelo learned something from Kobe in that moment. I'm sure Kobe learned many things from Carmelo, too.

Everything we saw in that first practice was extremely exciting for a coach. Our guys played some of the hardest, most energized basketball that I've ever seen. Every player wanted to send a message about what we could expect from him in Olympic play. Our coaching staff noticed that Dwyane Wade, in particular, brought tremendous energy to our team when he was on the court—a preview of the invaluable contributions he would make to our team throughout the Olympics. We knew that this was going to be a special summer for Dwyane.

The first practice also helped our players get reaquainted with LeBron's voice after having been apart for an NBA season. He communicated throughout. When going from one segment of practice to another, LeBron would announce the transition to the team. This is the type of communication you want from the bench to the court during a game. When a coach says something to a player on the court, you want that player to echo your message. LeBron did that naturally in practice. We may have just finished doing some work on our inbounds plays and I would say, "Okay, let's get going on some shooting drills off of our sets. Divide up into two groups and each go to a basket."

LeBron would immediately take control: "Shooting off sets, guys. White over there and blue over here. Let's go." This echoing of instruction is something that makes a practice run much more smoothly and is essential in games. Practice, then, isn't just about playing the way you will in a game, it's about communicating the way you will in a game. LeBron was like the emcee of our practice sessions. As a result, his teammates were reminded to be tuned in to the sound of his voice, a voice that would help guide them on the court throughout the rest of the summer.

Late July is a very busy basketball time in Las Vegas, as there are hundreds of high school AAU teams participating in several area tournaments. Many college coaches travel to Vegas to watch the young future stars in action. Additionally, Las Vegas is the site of some of the NBA's summer league games. By having our training camp there, we found ourselves at the center of the American basketball community. As a result, many high school, college, and professional coaches came to watch our practices, curious about what was going on with USA Basketball. Though our practices were closed to the general public, we always welcomed our basketball colleagues.

One day, Chuck Daly, the head coach of the Dream Team,

and Lenny Wilkens, head coach of the 1996 Olympic team, observed practice and spoke to our team. Hall of Fame coaching legend John Thompson from Georgetown, who headed up the 1988 Olympic team, also came to watch. John is a great friend of mine, but when I tried to approach him after one of the practices he said, waving his big hand at me and smiling, "Get away from me, Mike. You coach your team. I just want to watch."

None of the three former Olympic coaches were there to be noticed, they were only there because of their love for the game and their desire to see us succeed. There was something really neat about being surrounded by such greats from basketball past as well as the up-and-comers of basketball future. It situated us firmly in a position within the history of the game in the United States.

Moment: Johnny Dawkins Reaches Out to Carmelo—July 22, 2008—Las Vegas, Nevada

When we first began working as a team in 2006, we started out practicing twice a day, once in the morning and once in the evening. It was not too long before we decided that this was not the best way and we adjusted, deciding to practice only once each day. The driving reason behind this choice was the fact that we wanted to leave room for the guys to follow the routines that they do individually to keep themselves in game shape. Even when you are trying to bring a group of people together to act as one, personal time is important. You cannot forget to allow people opportunities to improve on their own, because individual improvement also means team improvement. I was impressed daily by the work ethic of the players. They would do Pilates or weightlifting before practice, then shooting or physical therapy afterward, everything that they needed to do to ensure that they were in peak condition. Some even traveled with their individual trainers. For them, practice carried over into what they did throughout the day. This type of thing is not forced improvement. *When people take charge of their own progression, they can become more vested and feel more ownership.*

There was no way that we could accommodate everyone's individual needs within our team practices. However, it was our responsibility to ensure that the players had access to what they needed for their personal improvement regimens. This, like everything else, meant coordination. Johnny Dawkins, my former associate head coach at Duke and the current Stanford head coach, did this for the National Team as the director of player personnel. Along with our trainers, he coordinated times, locations, rides, everything the players needed to facilitate their individual workouts. Because we had him specialize in this, over the course of the three years Johnny was able to learn about each player's individual routine and adapt to his needs. When you give someone the opportunity to specialize, they can become so adept at what they do that they develop the ability to anticipate. When people are able to anticipate, they can become instinctive. A goal in team building ought to be to have every individual so adept at what they do that they can follow their instincts productively. In his own quiet way, Johnny connected with each one of our players and became an expert in what elite players had to do to prepare.

Johnny's work was particularly beneficial to Carmelo Anthony. They formed a strong relationship over the three years. During the first two summers, Carmelo was arguably our team MVP, the leading scorer in both years and USA Basketball's Male Athlete of the Year in 2006. But, as we started out in the summer of 2008, Carmelo was just not quite as sharp as he had been. So, Johnny instinctively reached out to him and the pair did twenty to thirty minutes of extra game-speed shooting after every practice.

A lesson that any team leader can learn is that it is important to give everyone some autonomy. I did not tell Johnny what he should be doing with Carmelo on a day-to-day basis. He knew better than I did. Of course, as the leader, I did keep track of what they were working on together. I would watch and Johnny would tell me about how he felt the workouts had gone. Even though it is important for people to have autonomy to do what they do so well, you are still the leader and are responsible for knowing what is going on. I agreed 100 percent with everything Johnny chose to do with Carmelo, and I know it was a benefit to our team. If you have done the preliminary work of ensuring that your team is made up of all good people, why not give them some freedom to operate on the instincts they have developed? This kind of autonomy also helps to cement the pride that comes with ownership. Johnny knew that what he was doing was important, and the fact that I trusted him completely to do his job made it even more clear that this was not *my* team, it was *our* team.

Moment: A Bad Practice—July 23, 2008—
Las Vegas, Nevada

Not all practices are as exciting for a leader as that first one had been for us. On July 23, our team practice was quiet and our players were not sharp. They weren't competing at the same level they had two days earlier. I said to the other coaches, "We can't just talk about wanting the players to step up; we have to do our job and tell them when things are wrong." After all, we were the coaches. Ensuring that practice went well was our responsibility. When a practice does not go as well as it should, you can't just pretend it didn't happen. You have to address what was wrong and you have to fix it.

I wanted to take a step in the right direction immediately. I had promised our team that I would always tell them the truth and now I had to do that. I asked to meet privately with Kobe and LeBron. When I had them in front of me, I calmly told them what I thought. "I was not happy with that practice," I said. "It was disruptive. It wasn't tight. No one was talking."

Kobe responded, "Coach, I think we are getting disinterested." It was a natural reaction. Competitors want competition and get bored in its absence. Looking back over the practice plan weeks later, I recognized immediately that I was partially to blame for the practice's slow pace. On that day, we spent forty-five minutes explaining and instilling our team's zone defense before we stretched, because we had planned to practice zone defense and offense in our scrimmages against the Select Team. It was too much walk-through. We had been trying to create a habit of playing fast and defending hard, and all of a sudden I began a practice at a very slow pace. I should have done that differently.

But the fact was, people were going to try to slow us down in the Olympics and we were going to have to react. We couldn't allow a change in the pace of a game to affect how hard we played or how disciplined we were.

"You might be right," I said to Kobe. "But we can't be a team that just decides when we're going to turn the switch on. Our switch has to be on all the time." One of the standards we had established for our team was a standard of performance. We had told ourselves that there would be no bad practices. Bad practices are not the end of the world, and, most likely, they are going to happen from time to time. But in practice just as in games, teammates have to hold each other accountable because you play how you practice.

As our brief meeting concluded, I told Kobe and LeBron, "We're not going to have a long meeting before practice tomorrow. We don't need to talk. I am just going to say, 'We need to be in the gym, not here watching tape.'" When both guys nodded their approval, I knew that was the right move. The first line of the practice plan I wrote up for the next day read, "11:00–11:05—Team Meeting."

Moment: USA versus Lithuania Exhibition— August 1, 2008—Macau, China

Before leaving Las Vegas after the last practice in our home country, I told the team that I did not want them to consider this the end of our training. When NBA teams break training camp and begin playing in their exhibitions, there tends to be a different tone to their practices. We had found in 2006 that this happened to us when we left training camp in Las Vegas. We did not have the high quality of practices on that trip that we needed to win the World Championships. There was a mind-set that breaking training camp meant practices could loosen up.

So in 2008, we told our team prior to leaving the country that the practices and exhibition games that we would play in Macau and Shanghai would be considered an extension of our camp. In fact, those practices had the potential to be even more focused. We would be on foreign soil and it would be just us. No families would accompany us on that leg of our journey—not even my wife, who travels with me almost everywhere I go. This was not meant to isolate family and friends from our mission. On the contrary, I wanted families and friends to be part of our team, their presence enriching our experience. We would all look forward to their rejoining us when we got to Beijing.

But there is a time in team building for ultimate focus on the mission. The practices in Macau were the best, hardest, and most competitive we had, and they really laid the foundation for who we would be in the Olympics.

We considered the five exhibition games we played as practice, part of our preparation for our ultimate test. In addition to helping us raise the money we needed to cover our expenses, they granted us opportunities to face the type of international competition we would see in Beijing. Three of the five teams we played would be participating in the Olympic games. Our August 1 exhibition versus one of the teams, Lithuania, would be the culmination of our time in Macau. It was an important game for us; Lithuania had been one of the teams to beat our 2004 Olympic team four years earlier.

We won the opening tip and, right away, made our mark with a dunk from LeBron James. There was no looking back from there. After we grew our lead, Lithuania never came closer than nine points. The game ended in a 120–84 US victory over an excellent international team and a solid Beijing medal contender. Every one of our twelve players played eight minutes or more, and everyone scored. We played a terrific offensive game against Lithuania's zone, passing the ball extremely well and finishing with an impressive 34 team assists. But, in the most impressive statistic of the game, our players stole the ball 16 times, ten of our twelve players tallying one or more steals. The game was a testament to the dedication we had shown to taking advantage of our competitive edge. After that game, LeBron put it simply but well when he said, "I think as a team we got better. It's all about getting better." Indeed, that's what practice is all about.

Moment: The Scout Team—August 9, 2008— Beijing, China

Part of what makes practices successful is attention to detail and respect for the opponent. When we got to Beijing, there was no Select Team to scrimmage against and no further exhibitions to play. But we still needed to find a way to simulate what we would face in Olympic competition. Fortunately we had a staff made up of individuals who had been basketball players and we were able to form a "scout team" to run the offenses of our opponents in the half-speed walk-throughs that we would conduct the day prior to each game. Johnny Dawkins, Steve Wojciechowski, and Chris Collins—who had all played for me at Duke and professionally either in the NBA or overseas—were joined by Tony Ronzone, who had played at Long Beach State and overseas, and Chris Spatola, who had played at West Point.

Because they had all played the game, the scout team could pick up another team's system quickly and run it well. Additionally, by not asking any of the twelve members of our roster to play the role of the opposition, they were all given white jerseys. When we got to Beijing, it was important to us to have everyone on the team united, all with equal status. It also facilitated more focused preparation because no one had to learn how to run another team's offense while also learning how to defend it. Playing against the scout team meant that they were going against someone else, not their teammates. And it gave the seven guys who were not on the court at a given time the opportunity to practice communicating about the game plan with their teammates who were out there.

Practicing against the scout team also provided some opportunities for the coaches and players to bond. There were certainly moments of levity that occurred when the older and outsized scout team, in their too-short yellow mesh jerseys, went up against NBA All-Stars. On one occasion, Chris Spatola was matched up against LeBron James. Chris was a solid player and top scorer at West Point but at six feet tall and a lean 160 pounds, his matchup versus the six-foot-eight, 260-pound LeBron would be an unlikely one in basketball. Turning to LeBron before the play began, Chris said to him, "Tough matchup." LeBron acknowledged that the size differential might be a tough one for Chris. "No, I mean for you," said a smiling Chris, making LeBron laugh.

For the men who made up our scout team—men who hope to devote their careers to the game of basketball—these memories are irreplaceable. To know that they played a role in preparing our team for the gold medal is something they will never forget. As Chris Collins put it, "For a coach, what could be better than getting to work with those players? A lot of times I would lose myself in the coaching, but later, when I got back to the hotel, I would think, 'Man, where was I? I can't believe I was just matched up against Carmelo Anthony or that I was running drills with Deron Williams and Chris Paul.'"

And it was not just a coaching fantasy come true. The staff and scout team were crucial to preparing our players for their mission. They helped the players see their competition before they even took the court. The day before our medal-round game against Argentina, Johnny Dawkins played the role of Argentina's star guard—number 5, Manu Ginobili. It was typecasting. Johnny had been the Naismith College Basketball Player of the Year in 1986 and had a successful nine-year career in the NBA. And, like Ginobili, he was a shooter, a scorer, and a lefty. While play versus the scout team was supposed to be only half-speed, Kobe Bryant was all over Johnny that day, bumping him and playing stifling defense. No doubt, Kobe was going 100 percent. When practice was over, Johnny, at forty-four years old with a couple of bad knees, limped slowly off the court. Some of the guys got on Kobe's case, "Kobe, what'd you do to JD?" they asked.

"Sorry," he responded. "I didn't see Coach Dawkins out there. All I saw was number five."

Moment: Talking to Tayshaun in Practice— August 11, 2008—Beijing, China

Each of the twelve players on the Olympic team had great basketball knowledge; they knew what they were talking about. Part of being an effective leader in this context is realizing that the players can and should coach each other, like I had seen Kobe do with Carmelo on that first day of practice. Often they can notice things and elicit reactions from one another that you never could. They can also provide valuable input to the coaching staff. Mine was not the only voice heard in practice or at timeouts.

Throughout our time together, I always admired Tayshaun Prince as a true student of the game, and a darn good one. Whenever we would come into timeouts, he would pull aside the individual playing his position on the court and instruct him on things he had noticed while studying their play.

Even more than before, when we got to Beijing, I used practice as a time to reach out and interact one-on-one with players on the team. The day after our first Olympic game, I felt it was particularly important to single out Tayshaun. Though I think he already knew, I wanted to be sure he understood that I recognized his crucial role on our team. He played significant minutes, but not as many as several of his teammates. But this team would not have been the same without Tayshaun Prince. I had come to rely on his face when explaining something to the group. When something really resonated, he had a look of understanding and would nod his head. As we stood on the sideline during practice, I said to him, "You're really an intelligent player. I often see you nodding when something makes sense, and I appreciate that because it lets me know that I have explained it well. But I want you to also let me know when something doesn't make sense. I really respect your understanding of the game, so you let me know if I'm ever off base." Tayshaun said that he would do so.

In these talks, I always tried to explain to the players their roles on the team, roles that were almost always evolving. I didn't give them a static description of who they should be the first time we met. *Job descriptions, just like the practice plan, should be dynamic.* When you give time to a person and explain their ever-evolving role, it makes them feel good. It is a reminder to them that their role is important enough to warrant explanation. Being on the court while having these talks was also symbolic. This was the place where our communication with one another would be the most important. Practice is not only about preparing your bodies and minds but cementing your relationships within the context of what you are trying to accomplish, relationships in which your communication will be at its best in the environment where you do business.

TAKE THE TIME

Take the time to practice. In fact, take the *most* time to practice. Don't send your team into battle unprepared. Remember that competition within the framework of practice keeps it exciting and also makes possible individual improvement, which in turn makes your team better. Also try to find ways to simulate, with as much realism as possible, what your team will eventually face in pursuit of your goal.

In practice, you are working not only to improve on your weaknesses but also to build on your strengths. You should practice those things you need to improve upon in order to speak the language of the competition, but your practice should also be based on what you believe to be your competitive edge. Determine what it is that sets you apart from the opposition and use practice time to develop that ability.

Empower the leaders and other members of your team to be a part of the learning that takes place in practice. You, the leader, cannot be a part of every play, every interaction, that goes on. Allow others to specialize, then give them the freedom they need to operate based on their expertise. Encourage the members of your team to exchange learning and teaching with one another. This, too, creates more ownership and keeps people even more invested in your training.

While you won't be a part of every activity in practice, always have a sense of how it is going. If a practice does not go well, it is your responsibility to do something about it. You can't just dismiss a bad practice, because ultimately you and your team will perform the way that you practice.

A coach or leader must be prepared and have a plan for the way practice time will go. But, like so much of team building, the practice plan should be flexible, allowing you and your team to adapt to your needs as they develop. It is when you have the most control over who your team will become. Practice is the leader's time to shine.

TIME FOR SELF-ASSESSMENT

How can a team reach its potential if it cannot look at itself with a critical eye? The military does not simply train, go to battle, and hope that their plan has worked. A company does not merely create a business plan and stick to it no matter how their environment changes. There is always a need to evaluate performance in battle or in business and then retrain based on your assessments. In team building, self-assessment must take place both at the group level and on an individual level for each of the team members. This does not exclude the leader, whose individual self-assessment may be the most crucial of all.

Precedents are often good, but they can sometimes be extremely dangerous. They can make you complacent; you can fall into a pattern of just doing things the way they have been done before. This robs you of the benefits that come with constant self-assessment and critique.

On teams, self-assessment should take place not just from year to year or quarterly, but from day to day. In business, just as in sport, you can plan for a lot of things but you cannot allow yourself to become imprisoned by your plan. There has to be room for change. And when you recognize a need for change, you and your team have to be willing to make it. Improvisation and flexibility should coexist with planning and preparation. And, when you really think about it, it shouldn't be hard. You should always want to find ways to get better.

Becoming your best is an ongoing process. With our National Team, we learned every single day. We made little changes along the way like changing from conducting two practices a day to one after having discovered that our players would work harder in one good, long practice than they would in coming back together for a second. It was best not to micromanage and to allow our players time for their individual improvement routines.

Moment: Loss to Greece in FIBA World Championship— September 1, 2006—Saitama, Japan

I have never suffered a more devastating loss in my thirty-three-year career as a head basketball coach. When the final buzzer sounded and the scoreboard read 101–95 in Greece's favor, I made eye contact with Jerry Colangelo and did not know what to do. I said the only thing I could think to say, "I'm sorry. I'm so sorry." He had brought me on board as his partner in a mission of the utmost importance for the future of basketball in the United States and I had failed him. I had failed my country, my players, my family, and myself. I was at my lowest point. And I wasn't alone in this feeling. It was a rough locker room.

We lost to Greece because our team had never experienced a game of that magnitude in international competition. None of the early games we played that summer matched the intensity and tough physical play of that game. The matchup against the Greek team was the epitome of international basketball, and we had not yet learned it at a high enough level to win. Of course, all the praise goes to Greece. Their team was magnificent on offense. Their execution of the pick-and-roll was masterful. And their players seemed to hit every shot, connecting on their field goals an impressive 62.5 percent of the time.

Our team actually started out the game playing very well. In the second quarter, we were up by 12, and we had two chances to go up by 15 and then 18 points, but we missed on two crucial three-point shots. We did not take advantage of our opportunities and the Greek team, who was hardened in international experience, came back and took the lead at halftime.

In the last quarter we made our own comeback but were not able to close the gap. When the game finally ended, there was a feeling of real hopelessness among our team. But despite our crushing disappointment, we all knew that we needed to handle the situation properly and to give credit where credit was due. We shook hands with the Greek team, and I embraced my close friend and Greek head coach, Panagiotis Giannakis, whom I have known for the majority of my basketball life. I said to him, "Congratulations—I am very happy for you. I know this is an amazing win for you, my friend." And indeed, it was likely the greatest win of his career. But for me, it had been the worst loss.

No matter how I was feeling, I still had to face the press. Carmelo Anthony and I sat at a table in front of dozens of members of the media, knowing it would not be easy. It would be a tough audience, and it was Carmelo who was asked the first tough question.

"How much of a shock to the system is it to go out like this?" a member of the media asked.

Carmelo responded, "To lose any game is a shock to us. We came in with the mentality that we wanted to win this game and move on and hopefully win the gold medal. Unfortunately the Greeks came out tonight, especially in the second half, and went on a twelve- or thirteen-point run, and they never looked back. At the end of the day we've got to go back and get ourselves together; we still have one more game to play. It's not like it's the end of the world for us. We came into this thing together, we win together, we lose together, so that's how we've got to go out."

He made no excuses. He did not complain. And he recognized the Greek team's stellar performance. Even though he, individually, had scored 27 points in that game, he accepted responsibility for the loss on our team's behalf. In that moment, Carmelo Anthony was beautiful. No blame. No scapegoats. We felt the pain of that loss as a group. Even through that pain, we could see that our relationship and culture building was working because, while we were not yet ready to win, we were ready to lose *together*. By making it clear that we had collectively endured that loss Carmelo laid the groundwork for us to win together in the future. His grace in that moment guided our team's thinking going into our final game of the summer and set the tone for the task that still lay ahead.

In the months following that game and on into the staff and players' regular seasons, people were down on USA Basketball. They still did not believe that it could work. They didn't believe a group of NBA professionals could unite under a college coach. In all the numerous times our players and staff were asked about that loss, not once did anyone have a negative comment. Even though we were separated and engaged in our real lives, we hung together and revealed our strong character.

I left the stadium that night still very personally distraught. Later, in our hotel room in Tokyo, my wife watched me with a worried expression. She had never seen me more overcome by a loss. I couldn't sleep. I paced. I didn't know what to say and there was nothing that could be said to me.

And then the phone rang. It was my daughter Debbie, calling from back home. I could hear Mickie explaining to her that I was not in a good place and that she was at a loss as to how to help. When she hung up a few minutes later, she rejoined me in the living area of our hotel suite and conveyed a message from Debbie that turned everything around. "In every fairy tale," Debbie had said, "something bad has to happen. Otherwise, there is no happily ever after." Having been married for almost forty years and raising three daughters, I have learned that sometimes women have a way of expressing things that a man could never come up with. Debbie was right. The fairy tale would go on and our happy ending was not yet spoiled. For me, personally, Debbie's message was the first step back on the road to success in Beijing. That's what your friends and family can provide for you when you allow them to be a part of what you do.

I've always believed that failure can be an integral part of success. When you attempt something in which failure is possible, you test your limits. Failure requires you to reevaluate. The tremendous impact that the loss had on all of us led to the realization that who we were versus Greece could only get us to a certain point. To pass that point, we had to change who we were. When our staff was able to rationally analyze what the game had taught us, we knew we still had much to learn. At first I didn't see opportunity in this loss. I was too hurt. But this was the time for some much-needed self-assessment: a painful opportunity, but an opportunity nonetheless. This wasn't the end for our team. Carmelo Anthony and my daughter Debbie taught me that.

We were able to learn many valuable lessons through this loss in the World Championships, and I admire Jerry Colangelo's patience in giving us the chance to learn those lessons. He didn't panic. Even immediately following the game he said, "Our goal and our objective is to try to win a gold medal in Beijing, which is in '08. So we have a lot of work to do. We have to build on what transpired here. There were a lot of good things and there are some things that we are going to have to do better . . . Quite often, before you get to the finish line, you're going to have some knock-downs." He recognized the good that had been accomplished in our first summer together and had the strength and belief to move forward. He knew without having to be told that the fairy tale was still intact. Everyone needs someone to believe in them. In this endeavor, Jerry provided that unwavering belief for me. I knew that there was no blame and that any lessons to be learned we learned together.

Of all I learned that first summer, three things stand out. First, it taught us that we may not have the personnel quite right. We were too young and we needed to bring in some experienced players who would not be rattled by the very physical international play and who would bring to the team an understanding of legacy. Don't get me wrong—our 2006 team was extremely talented, and it was a group of good guys who worked hard and wanted to win. But we needed to find a different mix of talent, character, *and* experience.

Second, we had to assess the way in which we prepared. We had made a great attempt to learn the world's game of basketball on the world's terms, but we had not learned it well enough, and what we learned had not been practiced to the point of becoming habit.

Third, and I think most important, I learned a great deal about the way I had coached this team, what I personally had done wrong, and what I needed to change. From the beginning, we had discussed that we had to enter these three years without arrogance. In losing, I realized that I had been coaching with the same arrogance that I was trying to eliminate. I recalled that in one of our first meetings back in the summer of 2006 I told my team that we needed to remind the world of who USA Basketball was, and that in winning, we would reclaim *our* game. I had also told them that our goal should be not only to win every game, but also to win every quarter of basketball that we played. I regret having made both of those arrogant statements. And it was after the loss to Greece that it was truly embedded in my mind that this was not our game anymore. I had told that to my team and asked them to believe it, but until then I am not sure that I realized the entire truth of it. Basketball belonged to the world now, and I needed to see it for myself. I learned a lot. Only looking back do I realize how much.

So, as I assessed my own performance heading into our next summer together, I saw that I had gone from telling my team that we needed to win every quarter to not yet being qualified to compete in the Olympics. Only the host country, China, and the gold-medal winner in the 2006 World Championship, Spain, were automatically invited to compete in Beijing. Because of our loss, we were required to play in the 2007 FIBA Americas Championship and place first or second to earn our trip to China. We couldn't worry about gold medals—first, we had to get in the tournament.

We gained something else important from our loss: more time. And not just any time, but time with stakes attached. Without it, I honestly don't know if we could have come back together in 2008 and won the gold. Of course, we could not look at our loss to Greece at the time it occurred and accept it for all it would come to mean for our team. Then, it was purely devastating. But the self-assessment that followed led to action that was absolutely crucial.

Moment: Changing the Makeup of our Staff— April 23, 2007—Phoenix, Arizona

Our first summer together, Coach Boeheim, Coach McMillan, Coach D'Antoni, and I brought members from our respective staffs to Las Vegas to assist with our World Championship team practices. Part of the reason for that decision was that we had twenty-two players practicing with our team, where typically a basketball team has only twelve players. Having the Syracuse, Portland, Phoenix, and Duke guys all there allowed us to have multiple things going on in practice at the same time. We were able to get more repetitions for players in a shorter amount of time.

Another reason for the inclusion of those coaches was to have more guys who spoke the various languages we were dealing with. Having an equal number of staff who spoke the NBA language as those who spoke the language of college basketball allowed us to bridge our internal language barrier.

In May 2007, our staff convened in Phoenix for a meeting on how our second summer would go. I asked Jim, Nate, and Mike if they wanted to bring members of their staffs out for practice again. All of them suggested that we invite only the guys from my Duke staff. This was not to discredit the service that the other assistants had given us the previous summer; it was simply a change we decided to make based on our needs. One need that the USA coaches saw was to continue to ensure that I was comfortable coaching the team. They recognized that it was an adjustment for me to coach professional players. By having my Duke guys there with me, I could be more at ease. And, as a result, so could my USA staff.

We improved our personnel structure even more by pairing up one of my Duke assistants with each of the NBA coaches in conducting the scouting reports. This goes back, again, to making sure you are speaking the same language internally. Of course Coach D'Antoni and Coach McMillan are more than capable of putting together a thorough scouting report, but working with Wojo and Chris ensured that the information they gathered was presented to me in the manner to which I was accustomed. In a sense, Wojo and Chris were interpreters for us. They helped make certain that we, as a coaching team, were speaking the same language.

I loved my USA basketball staff. I loved the talents and knowledge that each coach brought to the game. I loved how up front we were able to be with one another. And I loved that there was never any jealousy or quibbling among us. But another thing that we recognized after that first summer was that we would be better served to keep Wojo and Chris with us for the entire summer. In 2006, they had been with us in Vegas but had not accompanied our team as we traveled to South Korea, China, and Japan. In addition to their utility in "translating" for us, we had found that our practices suffered without them once we headed overseas.

In forming teams, leaders come to learn that they are not the most proficient members of the team in all competencies. Jim, Mike, Nate, and I were all head coaches. It had been a long time since we had been in charge of physically conducting many of the drills a basketball team does in practice. Not only did the Duke assistants bring more youthful legs to the drills, they also brought their expertise. They kept up with the best and most up-to-date shooting drills, and they knew better than the rest of us how to run those drills in an efficient manner and how to keep everyone moving. Especially with NBA-level players, you never want guys to stand around. They want repetitions, they want constant action, they want to get the absolute most out of their practice time.

By deciding to keep the Duke coaches with us throughout, we picked up the level of practice. I could tell them that we needed to focus on certain things with regard to our shooting, like becoming more proficient in spot-shooting, or doing more work off the dribble, and they would know exactly how to incorporate that into our drills. As a result, every shooting drill we did when those coaches were around was intense, timed, and at game speed. We were able to have multiple activities going on at different baskets and accelerate the pace of practice. Because of the changes we made based on our honest self-assessment, our practices greatly improved.

Moment: After-Australia Meeting—August 6, 2008— Beijing, China

It is easy to recognize the need for self-assessment when you have suffered a defeat. That is what the Greece loss had done for us in 2006. It taught us that we still had not made all the changes necessary to win. It is far more difficult to recognize this need when you have won. *Winning can mask your deficiencies. But if the job of a team's leadership is to constantly self-assess, you have to be willing to look at yourself critically even in victory.* This is why we ended up having our most intense meeting the day after a victory over Australia. We won that exhibition game, but it had been our worst performance, and it was clear that we were not holding ourselves to the standards we had established together only seventeen days before.

I have said that our standards meeting in Las Vegas was *the* meeting. Well, this was the follow-up to that, and it was our toughest meeting. This was when we took a hard look at ourselves and asked, "Are we upholding our gold standards?" And I believe this is the fundamental point of self-assessment: discovering whether and to what extent you are upholding the standards that you have set for your team.

What we found was that in our most recent competition, we weren't. There were a lot of factors in the exhibition game against Australia that led to our team not performing at its best. It was our fourth game in six days and two cities and, since Australia was our final exhibition, our guys were already looking ahead to Olympic play. We had also wanted to give our players some free time before the Olympics, time we did not provide for our players in 2006. It was the right thing to do, but the lack of practice showed. On top of all that, the coaching staff had decided to use the Australia game to try some different substitution patterns and to test out some new things defensively.

But our first standard was "No excuses," so we could not use any of that to explain away our poor performance. The bottom line was that Australia had played well and we hadn't. We were sloppy, we weren't sharp, and we had allowed ourselves to lose focus on this game. No excuses.

That night, while still in Shanghai, our coaching staff, including Jerry Colangelo, reviewed the game tape. For about six hours together we analyzed our team's play and expressed to one another our frustrations and anxieties. Frustrations about the way we had played. Anxieties about going forward into our Olympic moment at less than our best.

We talked about personnel. Our team had some amazing pieces, but was our game plan putting those pieces together in the best way? We talked about leadership, both that of the players and our own. In short, it was a heated meeting. And it should have been. We were all about to walk onto the biggest stage of our careers and none of us wanted to lose—why would we hold anything back now?

Our self-analysis had to involve looking critically at one another and how we, as coaches, had led this team. At one point Nate McMillan said to me, "Coach, you have to be yourself." Initially, I was defensive. It was a tough thing to hear. But I realized that he was right. I had not yet had a meeting with this team in which I had been hard on them or called them out. For the most part, there had not been a reason to. But there was a reason now. In order to be myself I would have to have a tough meeting with them the next day.

I stayed up all night, first meeting with the staff and then, alone, thinking about what I would say to my team. I had to make sure I incorporated the concerns of my entire staff. I also wanted to meet individually with my internal leadership in Kobe, LeBron, and Jason. I love the concept of team and I believe that true teams are ultimately very strong. But a leader must always realize the fragility of relationships and the potential vulnerabilities that exist in bringing people together. Leaders of teams cannot be blind to those things. I needed to have a serious talk with my guys, but I also needed to think long and hard about what to say and how to say it. At the end of the day, Nate McMillan was right: I just had to be myself.

The next day, before leaving Shanghai, I approached Kobe at breakfast and asked if he would meet with me when he finished eating. My staff had put together a tape of clips from the previous night's game. Kobe and I sat together and watched, just the two of us, and dissected his performance. I told him that I felt he could have played better, that he had made some mistakes on both ends of the court. I said to him, "I need you to shoot when the shot is there. I also need you to realize that when you drive the ball, the other four guys are just watching you. There has to be more movement." Everything I said to him was supported by the video clips. When I finished, Kobe told me that he agreed and that he would work on the things we discussed.

Then I met with Jason. And, like I always did with Jason, I asked for his input first. "How do you think you're playing?" I asked.

"I'm not playing as well as I should be," he responded.

"Jason, we need you to assert yourself more. We need your leadership on the court. You're doing an amazing job off the court. But you are such a team-oriented guy that you are okay with Chris and Deron coming in and taking over. You're losing some of your player ego. I need you to be my leader again—on the court." Like I did with Kobe, I showed him some examples on tape. His footage showed some points in which his ball handling and passing were not as sharp as usual. And, like Kobe, Jason agreed and said he would be ready to lead in Beijing.

I met with LeBron last and his meeting was the shortest. I just wanted to make him comfortable with where I was going from here. "I talked to Kobe and Jason," I said, "and I showed them some things on tape that we need to work on. You may feel like you should say something to the team after last night," I continued, "but I want you to know that I've taken care of it. We're going to be ready to go." *Internal leadership is good for a lot of things, but the team leader is the one who needs to step up when it's time for confrontation.* I have never thought of confrontation as a negative. To me, it just means coming face-to-face with the truth. And, while it can be difficult, facing the truth is never a bad thing to do.

As soon as we arrived in Beijing, we had a team meeting before even settling into our rooms. It was our first of many in the Intercontinental Hotel meeting room. The timing of it was essential. We were about to enter an environment with a lot of distractions; we were about to get into a new routine that would last us the rest of our team's lifetime. Before any of that took hold, we had to refocus ourselves on each other and on our goal.

I opened the meeting with a highlight video put together by the coaching staff. The purpose of the video was to remind us of who we were and to present it in a manner that would get the attention of the players. It began with LeBron's speech from our standards meeting, reminding us all that we had to be a "no-excuse team." The highlights that followed showed our guys working together to create some beautiful basketball. The audio behind the footage was a song called "Hero" by Nas, interrupted intermittently by the voices of our players and coaches saying the things each had contributed to our gold standards. It was a creative way of reminding our team what those standards were and what we looked like when our play was governed by those standards. On the court, we don't perform as well in our offensive sets if we do not drill them. The video was a means for us to drill our standards. Just like anything we were trying to do basketball-wise, our standards needed to be constantly reinforced.

After the video, I addressed the team, and I was the most passionate I had ever been with them. I used language that could not be misunderstood and was right to the point. "Those are the things *we* said. Those are the standards *we* established for ourselves. And, guys, I'm not going to hold anything back. I am going to coach you and you need to be prepared to be coached by me. I will not let you down. This means that I am going to hold myself and all of you accountable to those standards."

It was a full-disclosure meeting, and I had to prove that I meant what I had said about accountability. Having talked to Jason, Kobe, and LeBron beforehand, I knew they were comfortable with my analysis of our Australia game, so they weren't taken off guard or made to feel defensive when I reiterated to the entire team some of the same things I'd said to them individually. It wasn't about embarrassing a guy or putting the blame on anyone—it wasn't about that at all. It was about showing our team that it was time to be accountable.

I could feel myself getting even more emotional as I concluded my talk. "My family arrives tomorrow, and I know that a lot of your families will get here over the next few days," I said to them. "My grandchildren aren't coming all the way over here to watch us win a damn bronze medal. They're coming here to see us win the gold."

We had all gotten back on the same emotional page. That's

the purpose of a meeting like that. You get to a point where you don't have time to have a less emotional approach and merely hope that a metamorphosis takes place. It's galvanizing a team all in one moment. I think they were really excited to see that I would do that, excited to see that I felt that level of emotion about them and about our mission. The After-Australia meeting allowed us to grow to a new level of emotional maturity. You could just feel that we were ready to win this thing.

Afterward, Jerry Colangelo came up to me and said, "Mike, you listened to all of our input last night, you heard everything, and you found a way to cover everything we said. This was a wake-up call for us. And you were the best you've ever been."

Moment: Changing Timing of Media Requirement— August 9, 2008– Beijing, China

When I say that self-assessment should be an ongoing process, I mean all the way up through your team's moment of truth. Many may think that once we arrived in China, we settled into an unchanging routine. While there is a great deal of habit in the way that you practice for competition, you can never become exclusively routine in your behaviors. We continued to ask questions of ourselves. How could we refine our team and our habits to get better? And you don't just assess yourself on how you do the major things, you examine the way in which you do everything. For us, self-assessment led to making a minor change in our practices that ended up making a major difference.

Whether you are in business or sport, addressing the media may become one of your team's responsibilities. While sometimes this can be a chore, especially when you deal with it a lot, it can also serve as an opportunity to tell the world what your team is all about. The coverage we received leading up to and during the Olympics helped us garner the public support that we needed to have. I really do appreciate some of the terrific things that were aired and written about our team and mission. But when your endeavor is being covered by the media, it is important that it never becomes a distraction from your ultimate goal.

One thing that was required of our team was that we allow the media to watch fifteen minutes of each of our practices and that we provide them with a thirty-minute window of access to our players and coaching staff. Throughout our first two and a half weeks together in the summer of 2008, we did this at the end of practice. What we eventually discovered was that our players were thrown off by this scheduling, because the end of practice is a time when players cool down and often do individual shooting and stretching. Allowing the media to do their work during this time was a distraction to the players. It did not allow them to prepare the way they would have liked, and it made the media's job harder because the guys would be trying to accomplish other things. After getting some feedback from the players, we decided to move this forty-five-minute period to the beginning of practice. Our guys still had energy, and they were able to answer questions enthusiastically while preparing for practice, getting taped, and stretching.

It really became a better setup for everyone involved because our guys were able to end practice in the way in which they were accustomed; plus, the media would get more out of the interviews because the players were in a better frame of mind to answer their questions. It was a very small change, and it was made near the end of our time together, but its effects made clear the need for self-assessment in all that you do throughout your entire time as a team.

TAKE THE TIME

Take the time for self-assessment. Remember the standards that you and your team established and try to fairly evaluate whether or not those standards are being upheld.

It's easy to force yourself to assess when you lose. Easy and necessary. It is harder when you are winning. Hard, but equally necessary. Self-assessment is not a thing that you do once in a while; it is something that should be taking place all the time. How can we do this more efficiently? How can we improve upon this product? Bottom line: how can we get better?

Self-assessment is communicating with yourself and refusing to lie. You end up living your standards more fully as a result.

TIME TO GET MOTIVATED

As a leader, it is your responsibility to put your team in the moment, to ensure that they understand what's at stake and the level of risk and reward. One of a leader's primary duties in team building is to sense this need for motivation among members of his or her team. It's about making sure, on a daily basis, that your team plays inspired, that they are at the level they need to be to fulfill your mission. There is very specific, focused motivation that takes place prior to your team's particular "tests," but motivating your team for your mission starts from the first time that you assemble.

Motivation is hard. It takes time and preparation. It is one of the everyday tasks of a leader. Remember, people are affected by the events of their lives. Being on a team can be fun and your mission can be exciting, but that doesn't mean that every individual walks into every team meeting ready to go. They may have had a fight with a family member, or been up late with a sick child, or been told some bad news. They may just feel tired. All of these things are natural and, of course, they will affect one's level of energy. You can't expect that people walk through the door fired up.

That being said, you, as the leader, had better walk in there ready to go. That's why leadership is not easy: it's your job to be at that level all the time. It is also your job to raise your entire team to that level.

I believe that a common mistake that leaders make is not motivating their best people. Some might think that superstars simply don't need this effort from you, that because they are the best, they are self-motivated. But that's wrong. Everybody needs to be inspired. And inspiring those individuals ends up being one of the most rewarding aspects of leadership. Imagine how good it would feel to help your best player become even better.

What you will find is that their positive reactions to your motivational efforts will serve to energize you. I had to adapt to coach this team, no doubt about it. I had to make some changes. But from the beginning, I promised myself that I would not change my focus on motivation. I could not just assume professional players would already be motivated. They deserved the best I had to offer. And I think they really liked it. Your team will appreciate your efforts because it proves to them that you see them as more than embodiments of talent. You recognize their ability to feel on a deeper level and the power their real emotions can have on their performance.

Motivation can come from many different sources, and great team motivation involves an effort to draw on all these sources. One source is reinforcing that sense of perspective that you taught your team early on. Another source is reviewing your established standards, giving your team the chance to see how they have performed based on those standards and how they can uphold them at an even higher level. Leaders who are talented at motivating teams can find new and creative ways to get everyone enthused about the mission.

Another element of getting your team motivated is rallying support from the outside by broadcasting your group's message. Of course, this starts with the obvious question: What is our message? *Typically a group's message is some combination of your goal and your standards: This is what we are going to do and this is how we are going to do it.* Our USA Basketball team's message was this: we want to win a gold medal and we want to do it in a way that brings honor to ourselves, the game we love, and the country we honorably represent.

Once you know your message, ask yourself: what is the best way to broadcast it to your audience? We have established that not all of the meaningful, motivational moments surrounding your team have to come from you, but sometimes they don't even have to come from within your team. If you create good outside partnerships and allow others to create moments, some amazing things can happen. As long as you are aware of who has been empowered to create moments and are comfortable with their motives, you can get so much motivation out of the things that others give to your team and the support rallied through their efforts. Like gaining perspective, broadcasting your message to the world can bring out a level of feeling in your team that could not be accomplished otherwise, a feeling that they have not felt for a long time or maybe have never felt. *Bringing about those emotions and harnessing the energy that they create is the essence of motivation.*

Moment: Magic Johnson Addresses the Team— August 2, 2006—Las Vegas, Nevada

In our effort to get our team prepared for their three years with USA Basketball, Jerry and I brought in a number of speakers whom we thought the team would respect and who had standards of excellence to which our players could aspire. The soldiers were a great example and brought that motivational sense of perspective. But we also thought it would be exciting for them to hear from a legend in the world of basketball, someone who had already won a gold medal. In his introduction of Magic Johnson, Jerry Colangelo mentioned that Magic was at the top of our list. And Jerry told our team that when he called Magic to ask him to speak, "Magic said he feels strongly about who we are and what we are trying to do." Magic's words would convey that message of respect for the cause, winning the gold, doing it right, and forging friendships through team building that would last a lifetime.

Magic began his talk with a statement of gratitude. "God is good," he said. "What a blessing it is for me to be here. Thank you for the invitation. This is a special moment, a special coaching staff, special players. If you look at it that way, you go in with that same attitude—this is a special time."

Hearing those words from one of the legends of the game, a three-time league MVP, twelve-time All-Star, and five-time NBA Champion really struck a chord. He had done some amazing things in his career but, as he put it to our players, "there are only so many people who get a chance to have the gold medal. You get a chance at the NBA Championship every year, but not this gold medal." An Olympic Championship meant the most even to him, who had accomplished so much.

He knew our mission well. It was the same mission that he and the rest of the Dream Team had been on in 1992, the mission that they accomplished so dominatingly. "You are in the same predicament we were," he told us. And while there is no comparison between our team and the original Dream Team, I understood the point he made. "We were the first Olympic team that they allowed to have NBA players," Magic explained. "The opposition thought, 'How are all those stars going to play together with one ball? How is this collection of NBA players going to come together for one purpose, one goal—to win the gold medal?' Our whole purpose was to prove everybody wrong."

We had to prove everybody wrong, too, and Magic told our players how to do so, "Remember this," he continued. "It's not about the offense because we have the best scorers right here in this room. You know what we said to ourselves in '92? We've got to do it on the defensive end. And that's what we talked about all the time." I remember thinking what a beautiful picture that was: twelve of the greatest athletes in the game, talking about defense all the time. I wanted to see it happen again.

Magic illustrated his point about defense with a great story. "The thing that woke us up was when the coaches brought in some of the top college players to go against us out in San Diego and they got up on us by thirty points." Magic looked at me, "Do you remember that?"

"Oh yes. I remember that," I responded. I recalled well the day that legends like Magic, Larry Bird, Patrick Ewing, and David Robinson were taken off guard by an extremely talented but young group of college upstarts like Alan Houston, Chris Webber, Grant Hill, and Bobby Hurley.

Magic continued, "Well, that was when we realized that we couldn't just show up. If we thought we were going to win just because we were in the NBA, we were going to get beat. And the crazy thing was, we came back, and we squeaked it out by about four or five points." He told our team, "That night, Michael Jordan knocked on my hotel room door and said to me, 'Magic, I was embarrassed. These college boys hung in there with us. Tomorrow I want you to be ready because I don't just want to beat them, I want to blow them out. It's going to start with D. And I'm going to pick up the point guard myself.'" I would remember these words the following summer when this generation's Michael Jordan—Kobe Bryant—expressed his commitment to defense by promising he would destroy every player he defended.

You could tell Magic loved telling stories from his time with the Dream Team. "The next day," he continued, "those college guys—they were in trouble. We picked up full court and played deny defense. By the time they looked up at the end of the first quarter, we were already up thirty. And we didn't need to talk trash. Our game would talk trash. We didn't have to say anything to them, because the nets were doing the talking. *Swish. Swish.*" The team laughed. That day it became about much more than showing up for the Dream Team, it became about taking pride in the way they showed up. They committed to doing that on the defensive end of the court, just as I hoped our players would do.

"It's bigger than us," Magic emphasized. "You have to take great pride in the fact that we're representing not only ourselves and our families, but—that jersey means something, something even more than the jersey that we wear for eighty-two games. After that, we were scrimmaging and playing against each other in practice like it was the World Championships. And do you know what that helped us to do? Carry it over to the way we played in games. Great practices: great games. So we went and blew everybody out because we played great defense. And it wasn't about us individually. It was about all the guys in the room."

That's when Magic spoke about the brotherhood that he formed with his Dream teammates. "The last blessing that I got was probably the greatest blessing and why I had so much fun," he told us. "I had to compete against Michael and Larry every year. And I always wished I could play *with* them. And finally that opportunity came, and I got the chance to get to know Michael Jordan the man and Larry Bird the man. You're not going to get this experience again, and by the time you look up you're going to be at each others' throats again because you have to go back to your teams. You get to know each other, hang out with each other, and play with each other for one common goal—and it's that gold medal.

"Now it's your turn," he told our team. "And us old-timers, we're going to be sitting back, feeling good watching you guys. Know that we're cheering for you, we're here for you, and we're supporting you.

"This thing is going to go quick. Take this as a blessing. Do you know how many millions of people are going to be watching you? Man, if I were twenty years younger, I'd be out there. I'd throw it to LeBron James and Dwyane Wade and Dwight Howard. Because I'm hyped right now for you guys."

Magic opened it up for questions and I asked the first one. "How did it feel," I asked, "when you all got your gold medals?" It was something I wanted our players to hear from someone who had been there before.

"Oh man," Magic replied, "I cried like a baby. You know that. It was an emotional time. First of all just to have the opportunity, and then to understand that we actually did it and I did it with my boys. It was the greatest moment of my life. I've won five championships in the NBA and I rank them high. But this was a different feeling."

After answering questions from some of the players, Magic concluded his talk by saying, "I'm proud of each and every one of you for giving up your time. You could be somewhere else, doing something else, chilling, relaxing. But you know what? You made a commitment to be here. You said, 'I want to be a part of something special. And this is definitely special—special team, special place, special time, special coaching staff, special man heading it up, now let's go out there and play special." It was beautiful to see a group of talented young men stand up and cheer for one of their heroes.

Having true icons from your field address your team can be an invaluable motivational experience. He or she will have instant respect from your team and will be able to speak directly to them in their language.

Moment: Presenting Our Fight Song—June 28, 2008— Las Vegas, Nevada

Publicity for your team and your message is important, and Americans love hype. It builds support for a cause, gains recognition for an endeavor. When I knew that I was going to be the national coach and I knew that Nike was going to be one of our major sponsors, I was excited. I realized that their people were the ideal ones to help us broadcast our message and earn public support for our team. I have had a relationship with Nike since I first signed a contract with them in March 1993. And, over the years, I have been consistently impressed by the creativity of the organization, top to bottom. When I found out that they would be a part of our National Team journey, Jerry Colangelo and I met with George Raveling, Nike's global director of basketball sports marketing, and I said to him, "We are going to really need Nike. We are going to need your creativity and expertise to help us make this America's team."

Of course, Phil Knight's Nike team was already way ahead of us and had already begun planning how to use their creativity and commitment to build love for our mission within our home country, where so often our loyalties are divided. I'm a Democrat / I'm a Republican. I'm a Duke fan / I go for UNC. I cheer for the Red Sox / I'm a Yankees fan. With our fan base united, we were able to feel the support of the whole country behind us.

One of the first ideas that Eric Lautenbach, my friend and director of college basketball sports marketing for Nike, presented to me was their concept for a documentary-style commercial that would feature our Olympic team. They wanted to set it to Marvin Gaye's 1983 rendition of the national anthem, which he performed at the NBA All-Star game. Eric played Gaye's performance for me in the conference area of our Duke locker room in the spring of 2008. He had been worried that I wouldn't like it because it was different, taking on the sound of an R & B song with a beat playing in the background. He thought I might have felt that it went against tradition. But he had nothing to worry about—I absolutely loved it.

Of course, I love tradition. But I also believe that imagination can act with tradition to produce something greater than both. Additionally, I have to remember when coaching my teams that tradition for me as a sixty-year-old is not the same as tradition for twenty-year-olds. Traditions don't just get passed from the leader to the team or from the old to the young, they get passed from all members of the group to one another. And sometimes they are created or re-created to fit your particular group. New traditions can be just as important as old ones, and creativity and tradition together can be a great motivational combination.

In their write-up of the concept for their commercial, the people from Nike had written, "Today, Marvin's National Anthem is a reminder of the historical legacy that this 2008 team seeks to uphold. It reminds them that they don't play for themselves, but for their communities, their heritage, their nation and each other." They wanted their camera crew to have access to our mini-camp practice and film the reactions of the players as we aired the footage of Marvin Gaye's "Star-Spangled Banner" for them in a locker room setting. I agreed with the overall concept for the commercial right away but added a couple of stipulations. First, I told them that they would have only one take. It was a great concept but we only had one practice in mini-camp, and there were many things that we had to accomplish that day.

Second, and more important, I told Eric that the team should be shown the footage on the court. I said to him, "What you've just played for me is our fight song. And basketball teams should hear their fight song on the court where they will play. Not in a meeting room or a locker room, but on our battleground."

So a few months later, at the start of our first 2008 team practice in Cox Pavillion, I called my team over to the sideline where a big-screen television was set up. When they had gathered in a semicircle around the screen, I said to them, "I just want you guys to see and hear something before we start playing together as a team, something that I want you to remember throughout the rest of our time together.

"Every team has a fight song," I continued, "a song that you hear that gets you fired up, that unites you. *This* song is our fight song. You will hear it before every game we play. And you will hear it when you are up on the stand in Beijing on August twenty-fourth with gold medals around your necks." Our players stood a little taller and watched with rapt attention. Their focus in that moment and throughout practice allowed Nike to produce a beautiful commercial. Either the sixty-second or the full two-minute-and-thirty-second version aired on NBC during every one of our games in the Olympics. NBC even had to reformat the way they scheduled their commercials in order to accommodate the full-length version. Following the Olympics, the people at Nike received an amazing e-mail from Marvin Gaye's widow saying that she had seen the commercial with her grandson, who had never had the opportunity to meet his grandfather but was able to watch him singing accompanied by footage of his heroes LeBron James and Kobe Bryant.

When it comes to motivation, impact is key. Every company, organization, and team has their icons, the things that define them. Seek out creative and personalized ways to present your icons and symbols. It's okay to look for twists in the way you present things, to be creative. Nike had come to us with an idea, and they were happy to let us use that idea as a means to motivate our team, not simply to promote their product. When you form good partnerships, people bring ideas to the table and you can work out ways in which those ideas can become mutually beneficial. By establishing the national anthem as our team's fight song, Nike and our coaching staff together set up the opportunity for our team to feel motivated every time our fight song played.

Moment: Team Visits Nike Olympic Basketball Exhibit—June 30, 2008—Harlem, New York

When we arrived in New York City for our one-day publicity blitz, our team was able to visit one of Nike's greatest tributes to USA Basketball. A storefront in Harlem was turned into a museum dedicated to the history of USA Basketball in Olympic play, and it featured our team. Beyond the entryway, which displayed the jerseys of all twelve 2008 Olympic players, there were some beautiful works of art to see. Two enormous 13' by 9' paintings of Lebron James and Kobe Bryant hung on the wall. LeBron's showed him in his USA uniform holding up an American flag, his head turned to the side with a serious look of purpose in his eyes. Kobe's pictured him in his USA uniform as well, but facing full forward, right arm extended with his finger pointed in the air, signifying the number one.

On one of the other walls was a work that the people at Nike entitled, "Moment of Silence," consisting of twelve varying basketball backboards, each framing a photograph of a basketball hoop somewhere in the United States. There was one in a gym, one on a barn, one in a city park, one in the middle of a field, each location serving to represent some aspect of our country's diverse landscape and culture. There were no people in any of the photos. "Where are all the people?" I asked Eric. "They are all watching the United States play basketball in the Olympics. That's why it's a moment of silence," was his response.

As if the remarkable, multimedia display was not enough, there were some gifts for our players as well. Each was given an iPod touch filled with photographs taken over the course of our two years together, as well as five custom songs written specifically for this team and performed by the hip-hop artist Just Blaze. Even better than that, they were each given a beautiful, hand-carved wooden box, painted a deep blue, engraved with their name, and adorned with an emblem on the top saying, "United We Rise." Inside the box, lined with red velvet, were the words, "We the people of the United States of America would like to present you with this specially designed uniform and footwear because we are honored that you have chosen to represent us as a team. You have captured the spirit of the United States and used it to create a new generation of basketball, a generation fueled by America's awesome determination and pride. We salute you as you accept the privilege of representing the United States in the games of the XXIX Olympiad."

The box was the perfect size to hold a pair of basketball shoes and a USA Basketball jersey folded on top. "We've had one of these boxes made for each of you with your names engraved on them," Scoop Jackson, the event's emcee, told our players. He called Jason Kidd up to the front of the room to accept his box on behalf of the team. "Jason, I know you already have a gold medal and a USA jersey. My question is, where are they?" Scoop asked.

Jason responded, "The jersey is folded up in a drawer somewhere and the medal is in a safety-deposit box."

"Well this time you will have a special place to keep those priceless items. The jersey will go inside along with your shoes, and you can display your gold medal draped across the top." Scoop walked the box over to an empty, spotlighted case, lifted the glass, and placed the box inside. "We will keep this here for you until then."

My wife told me later that she stood next to Chris Bosh as he stared at that box for about thirty seconds. "Pretty amazing, isn't it, Chris?" she said to him.

He looked back at her and said, "I'm just beginning to realize how big this is." This was his moment of realization. He was able to access a new level of feeling and see clearly that this was not about Chris Bosh; he was a part of something much bigger. Chris was absolutely essential to our victory in Beijing. If he had not learned that night in Harlem how big this was, could Chris Bosh have become the impact player he was for us in the Olympics? I'm not sure.

Sean Ford, who had been a part of three different Olympics with USA Basketball prior to 2008, told me that typically this moment of realization, when a player internalizes how big this is, comes at the Opening Ceremonies of the Olympics, when all the countries march into the stadium together. By that time, the weight of it all can become overwhelming, and it may be too late to properly prepare for a moment of this magnitude. We were given the opportunity to realize the significance of our endeavor before we even crossed the ocean. Nike helped us realize how big this was. And how good we had the chance to be.

The exhibit would remain open throughout the Olympics. Anyone who wanted to hear, see, and feel the message of USA Basketball could do so, free of charge.

Forming partnerships in the effort to broadcast your team or organization's message is a big part of team building. Make certain that you can go outside your own company's vision of who you are or who you ought to be and develop an understanding of how your group is viewed through other eyes. You may have a great idea, a beautiful message, or an outstanding product. But, how do you present it? How do you make it appealing, even to your own people? Part of the method USA Basketball chose was to collaborate with Nike, a company that already had a tremendous global vision and that could help USA Basketball play catch-up in the globalized world.

Moment: Team Photo at Statue of Liberty and Pep Rally at Rockefeller Center—June 30, 2008— New York, New York

When our team, dressed in their dark blue, matching custom suits, got into their places for our posed photo in front of the Statue of Liberty, there was a look of tremendous pride on their faces. After the photographer snapped pictures of the players by themselves, the coaching staff joined them. It was easy to stand tall and smile for those photos in front of the Statue of Liberty, knowing that we were going to be granted the opportunity to represent our country. As I stood in place next to Jerry Colangelo, I could overhear some of our players talking farther down the line. I heard Carmelo Anthony say, "Damn, fellas. We'd better win this thing." This was his moment of realization. This was when he recognized how big this was. Often when you take the time to broadcast your team's message, it becomes more deeply ingrained in the fabric of who you are. Your team can become motivated by your message all over again when they hear it anew, broadcast on a grander stage.

From the boat our team boarded buses to Rockefeller Center, where 1,500 people had gathered for a pep rally. It was yet another chance for us to earn fan support and another opportunity for our players to feel motivated by the purpose of our mission. Rockefeller Center had been covered with a beautiful hardwood basketball court, where our players would be introduced.

It had been a late night and a long day, and we were all exhausted. Taking a moment to rest in the green room before being introduced to the crowd, our players yawned and stretched—signs of fatigue that none of them would show once we were in front of the crowd. When the event's organizers told us it was time to go out, LeBron James quickly got up from his chair and began jumping up and down, getting himself psyched up for the crowd. When LeBron's name and jersey number were announced, he sprinted out onto the court, arms in the air, and created chaos in the end zone, where 475 children from local schools excitedly rushed toward him. Our players realized that this was almost as important as any game, rallying the support of our fan base. And we had to be at our best.

Several of the players addressed the crowd and took part in shooting contests with the children. It was a major moment of realization for all of us, because it was a time in which you could really feel the support of an entire country growing.

Moment: Doug Collins Speech—July 24, 2008— Las Vegas, Nevada

Our last speaker before leaving training camp in Las Vegas for our exhibition games in Macau and Shanghai was Doug Collins. Doug is a friend and the father of Duke Associate Head Coach Chris Collins. I love Doug, but that's not why I'm saying this: his speech was one of the most moving I've ever heard, and given our task, was most appropriate for this team.

In addition to being a great player and coach in the NBA, Doug Collins was a member of the 1972 US Olympic team. At that time, the United States was still dominant in international basketball; in fact, they had never lost a game in the Olympics. We were favored to take home the gold again, even though Russia had a team that was made up of much older, stronger, and more experienced players. Everyone knew they would be the United States' strongest competition. Doug had played his college career at Illinois State and was joined on the Olympic team by other college standouts such as Tommy Burleson from North Carolina State University, Bobby Jones from the University of North Carolina, and Ed Ratliff from Long Beach State University. As predicted, Russia and the United States met in the gold-medal game.

It was a loaded game, to say the least. Not only were we in the middle of the cold war, the tensions between the Soviets and the United States had begun to play out dramatically through sport. While either the United States or the Soviet Union had taken home the most medals of any country in every Olympics since 1936, Russian athletes were getting better and better, and were even beginning to take over events like the 100-meter dash that had typically been a shoo-in for the Americans.

It was an extremely physical game that remained close throughout. Down one point with seconds left to play, Doug made a great steal and drove the length of the court before being aggressively fouled on a layup attempt. He lay on the floor facedown for several seconds before he was able to stand and regain his balance. The US coach, Mr. Henry Iba, came onto the court to check on his player. Doug recalled that one of the assistants asked Mr. Iba who would take the free throws in Doug's place. Mr. Iba pointed at Doug and responded in his gravelly voice, "If that young man can walk, he's shooting the free throws." Still dazed, Doug stepped to the free throw line, where he would have two shots—two shots that the renowned sportswriter Bob Ryan described as "then, now, and perhaps forever, the two most pressure-filled free throws any American has ever shot in the history of basketball." Doug nailed them both and the US took its first lead of the game, 50–49, with just three seconds left on the clock.

Russia inbounded the ball, but there was confusion regarding a timeout that the Russian bench had attempted to call. Though there was one second remaining, the head of FIBA made the surprising decision to give the Russians their timeout and to actually put three seconds back on the clock, a decision that has since been found to be against FIBA rules. In the spirit of good sportsmanship, the Americans went back out onto the court despite the confusion. After the timeout, the Russian team inbounded the ball, and missed a full-court shot. The US team began to celebrate. Players, coaches, officials, and members of the media left their seats to join the victorious Americans on the court. But the celebration was cut short. An error had been made by the timekeeper and, much to the dismay of the American players and coaches, three seconds would be put back on the clock yet again and Russia would have another chance to score. Ivan Edeshko threw a length of the court pass and two US defenders, who were knocked to the floor, were unable to intercept. The Russian player Alexander Belov caught the long pass from the inbounder at the foul line, drove in for a layup, and scored. When the final buzzer sounded for the third time, the United States had lost by one point.

When FIBA denied the US team's official protest, the Russian players were given gold medals. Doug Collins and his teammates refused to accept the silver, believing, like Bob Ryan, that the game had been "a travesty, a joke, and a farce."

We showed the 2008 team a brief clip of HBO's documentary about this travesty called *3 Seconds From Gold*. Afterward, Doug addressed our team. In what proved to be an incredibly emotional talk, Doug told our team that he believed there are three types of people in the world: losers, winners, and champions.

He told us about the training his team had undergone in their effort to become champions: twenty-one days at the Pearl Harbor Naval Base barracks, practicing six hours a day. "Defense was our calling card," he said. "Mr. Iba wrote the number fifty on a chalkboard at one of our team meetings and circled it, saying, 'If

we can hold our opposition to under fifty points, we will win.'"
Mr. Iba's statement was prophetic. As it turned out, the final official score of the USA-Russia gold-medal game was 51–50. "That
experience taught me and my team a different set of international
rules," Doug said, smiling. "You play till they win."

Doug concluded by saying, "I know what I would entitle my
autobiography if I should ever write it: *Always a Winner, Never a
Champion*." Doug, through his tears, told our players of the opportunity we had to be champions—and champions on the highest level, Olympic champions, bringing home the gold medal on
behalf of the United States. "I remember the last song I heard prior
to that heartbreaking gold-medal game," he continued. "It was
David Ruffin's 'What Becomes of the Broken-Hearted?'" It turned
out to be a most fitting question for the team that walked off the
court that day never to claim their silver medals. "The song I want
you guys to hear last," Doug concluded, "is 'The Star-Spangled
Banner.'"

Doug would be on the Wukesong Arena sidelines in Beijing,
commentating Olympic play for NBC's broadcast. "When you
hear that song," he told our guys, looking out and seeing the
emotion on their faces, "I am going to take off my headset, stand
up, and sing it with you. And when it's over, I am going to look
at you and say, 'Thank you.' You will have become champions.
And once you are champions, you are champions together forever. No one can ever take that away from you."

That day, Doug Collins became a part of our team, too.

TAKE THE TIME

Take the time to get motivated. *Remember that motivation is not something that you simply hope occurs. It is something that a team's leadership must do, must actively work for, on a daily basis.* It takes time and preparation. Remember, all the members of your team are coming from their real lives, which may not always have them motivated when they walk through the door. Use your imagination and creativity to motivate. Motivate from different sources. And know that it's okay to form new traditions, ones that define your team.

When you work hard to motivate a team, that motivation comes back to you. The greatest thing for a leader to watch is the best become even better because they are inspired. The hungry look in their eyes makes you feel energized.

Take the time to establish what your message is. Try to look at it from all angles. Incorporate the assistance of other eyes so that you can become aware of what your team looks like from the outside. In forming partnerships, you can discover more about your team and its message. And when you broadcast your message to the world, sometimes it is your own team who will hear and understand it loudest of all.

GAME TIME

Competition has two purposes in the context of team formation. First, it gives you a platform for improvement. You can't reach your full potential without competition. This is the competition that you simulate in practice, the preparation you do in exhibitions or trials, and the subject material for your self-assessment and improvement.

Second, competition serves as a test for your team. The moments provided by game time are moments of truth. This is when you find out if you've made the most of your time to achieve your ultimate goal. Now you discover who your team became over the course of your evolution together.

When it comes to game time, there is another added element: pressure. How will your team handle it? Game pressure can do one of two things: it can inhibit you, or it can excite you. The inhibiting kind of pressure comes as the result of outside expectations. And, as I told our team in one of our early meetings, "We are not going to feel expectation; we are going to feel anticipation." Anticipation takes that outside pressure away and allows your team to feel only the pressure of the game itself, the kind of pressure that excites and brings out the best in you and your team. The type of pressure you should relish.

When game time arrives, your team has already spent a great deal of time preparing for it. All of your work forming relationships, learning the language, and getting motivated has been done with this time in mind. Of course, practice and motivational efforts throughout your team's life span prepare you, but there is also specific work that must be done in the twenty-four hours leading up to game time.

In sport, game preparation includes the essential step of presenting a scouting report. Scouting takes place in most businesses; you need to develop a thorough understanding of your competition. We had taken the time to learn the language of international basketball, but in preparing for games we needed to fully grasp the language of our specific competitor. What plays do they run? Who are their standout players? What can we do to disrupt their flow?

One thing that is important to consider is how and by whom that scouting report is presented. Remember your team's attention span and how essential it is to impart your message using your team's different voices. Also remember that you, the leader, are not necessarily the best person for every job. Who can communicate your game preparation messages to your team in the best way possible?

While you have certainly made efforts to motivate your team throughout, you intensify these efforts around game time. You have to inspire your team for *this* task, get them into *this* moment. Creativity becomes even more of a factor in game-time motivation.

Game time is when the stakes are at the highest level. It was time for us to find out if our preparation was worthy of Olympic gold. In each member of our team's lives and careers, this had the potential to be a crowning achievement. There are champions every year in the NCAA and NBA. But Olympic champions are crowned only once every four years. And on this stage, we were not playing for ourselves or Duke or the Lakers or the Heat—we were playing for the United States. Given our extensive emotional investment, we needed to go into our Olympic moment anticipating that each one of us would uphold our standards at the highest level. Game time is when holding one another accountable to your standards becomes most important. Living up to those standards meant a chance of achieving our Olympic dream.

Four of the games we played in the Olympics are superb examples of what "game time" means. All the elements were there: the high level of intensity, the possibility for feelings of pressure, and the extensive logistical and motivational preparation. These games tell the story of how time spent team building culminates in your moment of truth.

Moment: USA versus Greece in Olympic Pool Play— August 14, 2008—Beijing, China

As soon as Greece qualified for the Olympics at the 2008 FIBA World Olympic Qualification Tournament in Athens, we knew we would face them in our third pool-play game in Beijing. We were able to inform our team of the Greece matchup at our first meeting of training camp on July 20, 2008. They were all eager to face Greece again after having lost that heartbreaking game to them in our first summer as a team.

All six members of our 2008 Olympic team who had been with us in 2006 had looked forward to this game for two years. We had gotten over our loss in the World Championships, we had learned from it, we had used it to make us better. But we never forgot it. The great impact of that loss led to an increase in focus. Even those who did not play in the World Championships knew this game's significance.

The emotional investment required of us could never have been simulated in practice. You can have your scout team run the offenses and defenses of your opponent, you can be meticulous in your study of their habits, but you can't replicate the intensity of feeling. So this was our first real test. And its importance showed in the behavior of our team. There was total silence on the bus on the way to the game where typically there was chatter and laughter among the players. We knew that we would walk onto the court that night with people still asking two-year-old questions about whether we could play team defense, whether we could play a complete game, and whether our players had any heart.

Our intensity on the bus carried over to the court. We played like we had something to prove. After leading by only four points after the first quarter, we pulled ahead by 19 at halftime after a 31–16 run in the second quarter. That first half saw one of the most outstanding plays of the Olympics, when Dwyane Wade forced a steal and chased the ball down the sideline, saving it from going out of bounds by lofting a no-look, alley-oop pass to a breaking Kobe Bryant for a thunderous dunk. The play added both a steal and an assist to Dwyane's statistics and two more points to the scoreboard for our team. Dwyane finished with 17 points, five assists, and an incredible six steals in only twenty minutes played.

One of the best things about this game, and about the entire 2008 Olympic experience, was the emergence of Chris Bosh. For a coach, it is beautiful to watch the transformation of a player happening before your eyes. This took place for Chris on August 14. From the quiet persona he displayed off the court, suddenly an on-court warrior emerged. And that inner warrior was brought out in the moment we really needed him. As Kobe put it after the game, "Chris Bosh was terrific. He always seems to find himself in the right place at the right time, and when we penetrate he's able to find a little crack or seam and finish. Defensively he did a great job on the pick-and-roll and stopped their guards from penetrating. He was getting steals and we converted them into easy points." Chris let himself feel the moment just as he had at the Nike exhibit in Harlem. And the moment made Chris Bosh magnificent; he scored a team-high 18 points along with two blocks, two steals, and five rebounds. The Greece game was his coming-out party.

But what stood out most in that game was our team defense.

Chris Paul, who had played twenty-six minutes of terrific defense, said afterward, "This was a big game for us. We had this game circled for a long time once we found out what teams were in our pool. There were a few of us on the team who felt like we needed this game to prove to ourselves that we mean business and we're ready to win this gold medal. . . . We are built to play defense. Coach told us from day one that this may be the best defensive team he would ever coach, and it starts with us guards. As long as we keep pressure on the teams in this tournament, I feel like we will impose our will and eventually wear them down."

The final score was 92–69, and finally those two-year-old questions were answered. Could we play defense? The fact that we held Greece to 69 points and forced 25 turnovers was a good indication that we could. Could we play a complete game? Our intensity from start to finish said yes. Did we have heart? Damn right we did!

Moment: USA versus Australia Olympic Quarterfinal— August 19–20, 2008—Beijing, China

With five games of pool play behind us, we had finally arrived at the medal round, the round of one and done. In our pre-practice meeting the day before facing Australia in our first medal-round game, I wanted to have a serious talk with our players. "Today is August nineteenth," I told them. "On August sixth, our first day in Beijing, we had a very emotional meeting. An honest meeting. And now it is time for another one."

At that point in my career, I had coached 90 one-and-done games in the NCAA Tournament and 60 one-and-done games in the ACC tournament. But as noted earlier, our Olympic players were not accustomed to playing many one-and-done games because of the multigame series format of the NBA Playoffs. Entering the medal round, our team would be playing the equivalent of three Game Sevens of a playoff series, and they had to look at each challenge with the focus and intensity it deserved.

"We can take nothing for granted," I told the team. "Our record is 0-0 now. We have been good up to this point, but we haven't done anything yet. You may be reading that we have been dominant; the media is saying that there is no way we can lose. But not long ago I showed you an article where a reporter selected us to finish third. He said we don't have enough size and we lack continuity. People will say lots of things, some of them good and some of them bad. But we can't take any of that forward with us. This is *our* moment," I said emphatically. "Not anyone else's." Heading into our game-time moment, it was only about us.

"So, what *will* we take forward with us?" I asked them rhetorically. "Our character," was the answer, "and that character is best represented by our fight song." I took that opportunity to play for them the documentary-style commercial that Nike had made from our first practice, in which we had presented Marvin Gaye's singing of "The Star-Spangled Banner" as our team fight song. Though it had aired for the television audience back home, our players had not yet seen it. At its conclusion, I looked at my team and said, "It is not about what anybody *says*. It's about what we *do*. Champions *do*."

Nate McMillan and Chris Collins had prepared our scouting report for Australia, so, as was our custom, Coach McMillan presented the report to our team. He talked about the hot shooting of Australia and how we really needed to be assertive defensively, not by pushing and shoving but by putting exhaustive defensive pressure on their players. The way Australia was playing coming into the medal round, I thought they could beat anybody. In addition to their great shooting, they had a high level of confidence. In fact, I believe that Australia was likely the next best offensive team in the Olympics, averaging over 90 points a game. They had what you call a "shooter's chance," meaning that if you have good shooters in the game of basketball, you always have a shot at winning. Nate concluded by saying, "This is when we should be our hungriest." That was the only way we could counter Australia's aggressive style and hot shooting.

When a group of people are granted the time necessary to

become a team, certain phrases that define you as a group can develop. These are your inside jokes, your inspirational phrases, your collective mantras. Some of these come from the staff and are said in order to instill a particular mind-set; others come from among the players, things we may have overheard them say to one another that become central to who we are. While these key phrases are something that arise naturally, there is nothing wrong with incorporating them into a more focused strategy for motivation. And so we made it a practice to have one of our phrases printed out and placed on the seat backs of our team bus. What better way to remind us of the agreements we had made with one another and the identity we had formed than to use *our* words?

On our way to practice the day before the Australia game, those seat-back signs echoed one of the messages from our meeting: "Take Nothing For Granted (We Are 0-0)." Everything we had accomplished up to this point meant nothing now, and each of the eight teams remaining had an equal shot at becoming an Olympic champion.

On the day of our first game in the medal round, we showed a video to our team. It was another highlight video set to music, similar to the one we had shown at our meeting when we first arrived in Beijing. But this time we were able to use recent highlights from Olympic play. The song we used was "One," written by Bono and performed by Mary J. Blige with U2. The first shot of the video was a scan of our players lined up on the court, listening to the national anthem before one of our games. Hands over hearts, unified. The footage contained some spectacular basketball highlights: a LeBron blocked shot, a Carmelo three, a Chris three-point play. Of course, it included Dwyane's incredible alley-oop to Kobe from the Greece game. The dazzling basketball plays were interspersed with footage of the players celebrating together, showing their emotion for our mission.

When Bono first sang the words "One love," the video showed a close-up of the red "USA" across the front of Carmelo's uniform; when Mary J. Blige first sang, "We get to carry each other," it showed our players coming in for a huddle at our bench; and when Bono and Mary J. Blige sang in unison "One love," our team united at center court with their arms extended in the air after one of our victories. As the song faded out, a waving American flag appeared on the screen, and when Mary J. Blige's voice came back in with the song's concluding "One love," the video froze on LeBron's index finger extended in the air, signifying the song's title. I looked at the faces of the guys on our team when the video ended and I knew it had worked. It put them in the moment.

"Well, I didn't wake up motivated," LeBron said. "But I am now." What a great feeling for a leader, to know that you have been successful in getting your team motivated. It is invigorating. One thing that I learned from their reactions to these efforts was that the more mature your team is, the better they are able to embrace the emotion that accompanies group motivation. Especially with a group of men, it requires a high level of individual security to allow yourself to become emotional. These guys had it.

We put two signs on our bus that day: one on the way to the shootaround and one on our way to the game. The first read, "Defense: Five Guys Attacking as One," and the second read, "They Are in Our Way: Crush Them."

We played tight in the first half. Our guys were nervous and we couldn't find our flow in the first quarter, which ended with us leading by only one point at 25–24. Things picked up for us in the second ten minutes, concluding with a Kobe Bryant offensive rebound and put-back. Then Deron Williams hit a three-pointer just before the buzzer that put us ahead, 55–43, and changed the momentum of the game.

At halftime we made a few adjustments, the main one being that we started switching on defense in order to stop their penetration and better guard against the three. The fact that these adjustments got us off to a terrific second half showed something about who we had become. I think Kobe phrased it best when he said, "You know a group has become a team when you can make adjustments on the fly."

We came out ready in the second half, scoring 14 straight points, including nine off of three-pointers, to complete a 19–0 run that had begun in the last two minutes of the second quarter. Every one of the twelve members of our team scored in the game, and five ended up in double figures as we handled the feisty Australians with a 116–85 victory.

Moment: USA versus Argentina Olympic Semifinal— August 21–22, 2008—Beijing, China

On the day before the semifinal against Argentina in our pre-practice meeting, I reminded our team that we had been in this position before. "Two summers ago at the World Championships," I told them, "we were in this same situation. We were preparing to play in the semifinal game against Greece. But we are a hell-of-a-lot-better team now." We were different from what we were back then, and not merely because of personnel changes. We had grown into something better and stronger through our time together. We had learned about the game and each other, and we had developed a set of shared instincts. "We need to talk to one another," I told them. "We were quiet in the first half against Australia yesterday and that hurt us. If you get tired or nervous, talk more. It will keep you from falling victim to fatigue. When we're talkative, we create our own background music."

We decided to show another video on that day. This one would be set to our "background music," the music we made on the court, the voices of our guys. So we showed three and a half minutes of clips from various interviews with our players, all of them talking about our goal: the gold medal. Carmelo Anthony saying, "Our one focus is just the gold medal, nothing else." Carlos Boozer saying,

"This is what we dreamed of as kids. I get chills on my arms. I get excited. We'll always be able to look back on 2008 in Beijing and how we won the gold medal together." Michael Redd saying, "You're fighting for your country, you're fighting to win the gold medal: the most prestigious award we can all have in our careers." And ending with Kobe Bryant saying, "When I'm going to the grocery store or going to pick up coffee, people just come up to me on the street and say, 'Bring back the gold. Bring back the gold medal for *us*.' I saw a guy with a Celtics jersey at Disneyland and I'm ready to kill him. He's wearing a Garnett jersey, and I'm thinking he's going to say something smart to me about the Finals. Instead, he says, 'Bring back the gold for us.' Enough said." Exactly, enough said.

Mike D'Antoni had done the scouting report for Argentina along with Steve Wojciechowski, so Coach D'Antoni was the one who would talk about their personnel and style of play. He began his presentation with what I thought was the most fundamental point in playing against Argentina. "They won't beat themselves," Coach D'Antoni told our team. "Their hearts are too big. We are going to have to beat them." Argentina is a team that rises to the level of the competition. We knew they would play their big hearts out against us.

One of the focuses in our game plan was defending Manu Ginobili, who had averaged 17 points in his twenty-five minutes per game in the Olympics. Johnny Dawkins can attest to the fact that ever since Kobe asked me to do him a favor and allow him to destroy the opposing team's best guard, he had anticipated this matchup. Kobe would start out guarding Argentina's number 5. Dwyane and Deron would have their turns, too—but everyone on the court had to prepare to have an awareness of Ginobili throughout the game. As we talked about our defense, several of the players provided their input.

"If you make Ginobili play in a closet, he becomes a different player," said Kobe, our defensive stopper. "If there's no communication, we're going to get burned every time," said

LeBron, our vocal defensive leader. It was exciting to hear how invested the guys had become in our team defense. And I was anxious to see how that would manifest itself in our semifinal game against Argentina, the reigning Olympic champions.

In the post-game press conference after the quarterfinal game against Australia, Kobe had made a terrific statement: "We want to play against the best. We want to play the defending champs. It's all about challenges, and obviously we welcome all comers. Argentina is the defending champ. You want to be able to play the guys who won it the last time."

I concluded our team meeting with a similar sentiment. "Tomorrow will be a tough contest," I said. "But to be champions you have to beat champions. And we should go into tomorrow with tremendous pride and confidence."

On August 22, the day of our semifinal game, I told my staff, "We've waited two years to play this game against anybody, and we are so lucky we get to play it against Argentina. We have the opportunity to play in a great game tonight. *This is the time.*"

When the team came in, we went through a review of the scouting report. Coach D'Antoni reminded us that Argentina's guard, Pablo Prigioni, had only two turnovers in Olympic play. He told us about how their three-point shooting gave them life. And he emphasized Luis Scola's tough, physical play. But he concluded by reminding our team of the most important thing when you're playing against Argentina: "If you give them a chance, their heart just gets bigger."

We had one last video for our team. Produced by Nike's US general manager for basketball, Michael Jackson, this one was set to Ray Charles's version of "America the Beautiful" and was created solely to inspire the USA Basketball Men's Senior National Team. This magnificently produced video would be aired one time and one time only, in our team meeting room prior to our game against Argentina, the game we had to win to earn the chance at a gold medal. In some ways, it is unfortunate that no one else will have the chance to see the video, but in other ways it's really pretty neat to think that it was made just for us, and we are the only ones who will have the memory of watching it together on that special day.

Charles begins his version of the classic American song with what is typically sung as its third verse before singing the more well-known first verse, opening with the lyrics, "Oh beautiful, for heroes proved / In liberating strife / Who more than self, their country loved, / And mercy more than life." With Ray Charles singing those words, the video showed images of the landscapes and monuments that define the United States. As each iconic piece of Americana came on-screen, the images dissolved into footage of our Olympic team in action.

The highlights continued, overlaid on the waving red and white stripes of the American flag as Charles sang passionately, "America, sweet America, / You know, God done shed his grace on thee." And, in my favorite moment of the video, a close-up of the Statue of Liberty appeared with the lyrics, "He crowned thy good," and pulled away from the close-up to a wide angle showing our team, in their blue uniforms, posed on our boat in front of the statue as Charles continued, "with a brotherhood . . ."

As the song concluded with "from sea to shining sea" and the chorus repeated in a way only Ray Charles could sing it, the footage continued with highlights and emotional shots of our team playing on the court, celebrating with one another, bowing their heads during the national anthem, and, finally, coming together at midcourt for a huddle. The video truly captured the essence of our team, the fact that we were, indeed, a brotherhood, and that we were humbly representing the great country we all loved. It was a powerful representation of both the love of country and the love of the game that we hoped our team had come to represent.

When the video ended, I spoke to my team about how we would be remembered. "No one will remember who scored the most points for this team. Do any of you know who the leading scorer of the Dream Team was?" No one answered. "It was Charles Barkley. And he came off the bench," I responded. "But no one will remember any of that individual stuff. They will only remember that we were Olympic champions."

On the bus on the way to the game, there were signs at each seat reinforcing to our players, "This is OUR moment."

Prior to taking the court to warm up for our moment, we waited in the tunnel outside the locker room. After a few minutes, the Argentine team entered the tunnel as well. It was as if our team wasn't even there. The Argentine players formed a huddle and began jumping and singing in unison. It wasn't for show. It wasn't for television cameras. It wasn't for anybody but themselves. It was one of the most profound displays of spirit I have ever seen. I leaned in to Coach D'Antoni, who was standing next to me and said, "That right there is what international basketball is all about." After three years of studying the international game and learning its language, it was in that tunnel that I finally came face-to-face with its soul. When Argentina was playing, their whole country was playing. That was what we had to beat. Not their offense. Not their defense. *Their spirit.* It was at that moment that I finally understood who our opponent really was. And I have to admit, I was scared.

We started the game strong, jumping out to a 30–11 lead at the end of the first quarter. But, in that first ten minutes, Manu Ginobili went out of the game with an ankle injury and did not return. When you have practiced so intensely to face a particular challenge and something changes, it can throw you off. We had prepared to play against Argentina with Ginobili. We were not prepared to play them without him. After all of our work, his injury rendered us unprepared for the team we faced. It took a second quarter in which we were outscored 29–19 to wake us up. A strong second half ensured that we would come away with a victory. But, interestingly, we outscored Argentina the most in that first quarter when Ginobili was in the game.

Carmelo Anthony, who had consistently been our best player in the summers of 2006 and 2007, had not played his best yet in 2008. But the extra work he had put in paid off, and against Argentina he was outstanding. He played the most minutes for us that game—thirty—scoring 21 points and hitting a US Olympic record 13 out of 13 free throws. But it took a total team to beat Argentina, and our stats proved it was a real team effort: 15 points from LeBron, 12 each from Kobe, Dwyane and Chris Paul, an 11-point and 10-rebound double-double from Chris Bosh, 10 points and nine rebounds from Dwight Howard, and seven assists from Jason Kidd.

Jason came through again, and not just in his stellar passing performance. He also helped our guys keep their poise throughout the physical game. He was our leader on the court in that game, just like I'd asked him to be after our Australia exhibition. In the locker room afterward, it was Jason who I went to first, congratulating him on his performance. He had pulled our team together when Argentina came within six points near the end of the first half. "This is why I'm here, to keep everyone's composure," he said to the media. "Those other games were dress rehearsals; these are the ones that count."

The game was a great example of international basketball and the Argentines, despite the loss of their leader, played with the indomitable spirit that I had witnessed before tip-off.

Moment: USA versus Spain Gold-Medal Game— August 23–24, 2008—Beijing, China

The day before the gold-medal game, our staff found out that one of Spain's top guards, Jose Calderon, was injured and would not be able to participate. Before our team meeting, I pulled Jason aside and told him the news. "But we can't let up as a result," I said. "They have other good guards who will step up and play hard."

"We learned our lesson last night, Coach," Jason replied, referring to the loss of Ginobili the night before.

When Jerry walked in the meeting room he said a very enthusiastic "Good morning!" Even though it was 1:30 in the afternoon, it felt like morning for a lot of us. We didn't leave the arena after our Argentina game until after 1:00 a.m. The staff had been up until 5:30 in the morning watching tape and beginning our preparation for Spain. But he had the "good" part right. The day before you play for a gold medal is a good day.

As our players began to assemble for the 2:00 p.m. meeting, there was tremendous anticipation in the air. When Dwyane entered he told me that he had a difficult time sleeping because he was so excited. Chris Paul even brought his personal video camera with him to document the special day. But then Tayshaun made a point to come over and in his uniquely quiet way, said to me, "Coach, I think we need to have a serious practice today."

I agreed.

"In twenty-four hours, we will be playing in the gold-medal game," I told my team. "Game day" is a full twenty-four hours, not just the day of the actual game but the twenty-four hours preceding game time. Since our Spain tip-off was at 2:30 on Sunday afternoon, our focused game prep had to begin on Saturday afternoon. The gold-medal matchup would be our first and only afternoon game in the Olympics, and that would require an adjustment for us. The worst mistake we could make would be to wake up on the morning of August 24 and not be ready. There was simply not enough time before tip-off to wake up unmotivated.

I had thought long and hard about how to motivate my team going into our last twenty-four hours together. I joked with them, "It is my responsibility to put you in the moment. In trying to figure out what to say to you this morning, my first thought was that I would come in here wrapped in an American flag, rip it off, and be wearing a star-spangled Speedo underneath." The players laughed, and a few groaned in disgust.

"I decided against that," I told them. In a more serious tone, I continued: "Some really good things have gone on here. And we have built a foundation for USA Basketball. The main thing we've been during this time is honest. And to be honest with ourselves, we have to say that for one quarter last night, we didn't play well. We didn't meet our standards. Let's make tomorrow not just about winning but about living our standards."

I wanted to make the players recognize what a singular memory the following day would be in their lives and careers. "When you have great experiences in life," I said, "you always want there to be a photograph. You will watch the gold-medal game many times. It will be a forty-minute picture that will last you the rest of your lives. We want to be at our best in that picture."

I also wanted to set a tone of reverence for the day that followed. As Tayshaun had said, we needed to have a serious practice. It would be a short one without much movement because of the late night against Argentina and the early game the following day, but it would be a focused one. NBA players play basketball almost every single day of their lives. Practice becomes so routine for them that they have to do things to make it interesting. For a lot of the guys, they make practice more fun by taking half-court shots and trying other trick shots. And I really do not have a problem with that. But on that day, I didn't think there was a place for it in our team's practice. "Let's not take any half-court shots today or any of that stuff," I said. "Let's treat this twenty-four hours with dignity. Let's practice like we're going to play." I remember making eye contact with LeBron after I said this; he was nodding in agreement.

When we got to practice I told the team, "I want your mind. I want your body. And I want your heart. We need all these things to win." But that practice was more about getting their minds in the right place than anything physical. Their bodies were already there. I told them that if we could get in the right mind-set, we were going to play great. Adjusting to the change in game time was more of a psychological adjustment than a physical one. Since August 23 was Kobe's birthday, we also had a terrific moment at the end of practice, when his wife and two young daughters brought in a cake and we all sang "Happy Birthday" to him. Though I don't know it for a fact, I think I can guess what Kobe wished for when he blew out the thirty candles.

After practice, I talked to the team about whether or not we would attend the US women's gold-medal basketball game that night against Australia. The team made the decision that they all wanted to go together despite the 10:00 p.m. tip-off. It was a show of support that they wanted to give. Like they had in their trips to the Olympic Village and in supporting other US teams and individuals in Olympic competition, our guys recognized that they were a part of the bigger American team. Our bond with the women's team was particularly strong since we had shared a home with them and their families over the preceding two and a half weeks at the Intercontinental Hotel.

The US women played very well, and when they pulled ahead 77–56 early in the fourth quarter, our players were able to get back to the hotel a little early and get some rest. Attending the game was the best thing they could have done. Our guys stayed together as a team that night and were able to witness a gold-medal basketball game and the gold-medal-worthy play of the US women, who had dominated throughout the Olympic Games.

The next morning, our team would meet at noon. Prior to their arrival, our staff gathered for the last time. There was a buzz of electricity among us. "You have to think our guys are going to play great today," I said to them.

Wojo was the first to respond to me. "Right. You think about the investment they've made leading up to this. And here they are, on the absolute biggest stage."

Nate McMillan spoke up, too. "Right from the start of the game, we have to be together and be tough. We've done three years of preparation for forty minutes of basketball."

If we are to look at game times as moments of truth, to what truth are we referring? I believe that the truth discovered in game time is the truth about who you are as a team. Your character is revealed. At these moments you have to believe that you are prepared to become a champion. We didn't need to change things for the big game. We had already been doing the things that we needed to do to win, and we had been doing them at a high level. Why would we change now? A moment of truth can motivate you and lift you to play even harder, but it shouldn't change you. So, when the team came in and took their places, my message was simple. No bells. No whistles. I simply said, "This is it, men. Let's be ourselves."

Nate McMillan then took our team through some reminders from the scouting report. "Be tight and be connected," he told our team. "Spain comes into this game second in the Olympics in steals. Take care of the ball."

I added to Nate's comments by telling the team to play aggressive defense, pressuring the ball and attacking passing lanes. I told them to run, run, run—play the game to exhaustion. "The coaching staff will carry you to the bus after the game if need be," I joked. "Let's go after them with five guys. Let's be relentless." I wanted to remind the team of our standards and what it meant to uphold them, but I wanted to do so implicitly, by simply reminding them of the way we had already lived—and won—together. "Nothing new here, fellas, let's just be ourselves for forty minutes."

What more motivation does your team need than your ultimate moment? A lot of people think that this is the time to give your Knute Rockne–type speech. You have been creative with your words and motivational strategies throughout your time together, but now the moment itself is what lifts you. I concluded our meeting by simply saying, "Let's go win the gold." The simplicity of our message for that day was reiterated on the signs we had waiting on our team bus. They read, "Play hard. Play smart. Play together. 40 minutes from gold."

Before every game I have ever coached, I have made handwritten notes for myself about the other team's offense against our defense and, conversely, their defense versus our offense in sort of a move-countermove format. I have found that writing these things down—even things I've already heard my assistants say or have seen in the scouting report—cements them in my mind. *Committing it to paper commits it to memory*. These notes are for no one else but me. At the bottom of each page, I typically write in all capital letters something in particular that I feel will be a key for that game. For the Spain game, the phrase at the bottom of their defense versus our offense page read, "BE WHO YOU ARE FOR 40 MINUTES" and at the bottom of the their offense versus our defense page I wrote, "TALK TO *US*." We knew how to play; we knew what it took to become champions. Now we just had to execute. We had to keep ourselves focused and united through our system of communication. We couldn't allow ourselves to become distracted by engaging with the other team or the officials. Spain would certainly try to find ways to take us out of our game. Our team talk would combat against that.

The notes I write are my way of coaching myself. I lay them out in front of me and study them in the locker room before taking the court. I will read about a particular offense of the other team, close my eyes, and picture them running the play in my mind. Then I will picture us doing the things we have practiced to defend against it. In a way, I play the game out in my head before we even take the court. If it goes the way it does in my mental preview, I know we will win.

Those notes help me to not be distracted and to concentrate on what we have to do to be successful. I even refer back to them at halftime. On August 24, when I studied my notes before the gold-medal game, I was reminded to think only about beating Spain. Don't look at the American flag too long. Don't get caught up arguing with a referee. Don't think about the magnitude of it all. I had to resist those distractions as well as the other standard distractions that worry all coaches: that someone will get injured or that key players will get into foul trouble. Studying my notes helps me focus solely on the task at hand. And this was a moment for ultimate focus.

Fifteen minutes before game time, I watched as Spain warmed up. In basketball, you watch teams warm up hundreds of times. You look to see if that team appears ready to battle. Are they intense? Are they nervous? Are they loose? You try to get a feel for how they will play by observing how they warm up. That day, I noticed that Juan Carlos Navarro for Spain had a different look about him. He wasn't having a great Olympics to this point, averaging only five points a game on 13 of 51 combined shooting. But that day, he had a look of assuredness.

At ten minutes prior to game time, each team's head coach must sign and turn in his starting lineup to the officials. I typically turned mine in well before the deadline, since we kept the same starting lineup throughout the 2008 summer. But with ten minutes to go before tip-off, I would always go to the scorer's table to check the lineup of the opposing team. Sure enough, the roster showed that Navarro would be starting for Spain instead of Rudy Fernandez. I knew he would have a big game for them and that Fernandez would be fired up coming off the bench.

In international play, all team members are introduced prior to tip-off, not just the starting fives. Following the introductions that day, the two teams stood on the court and respectfully listened to each country's national anthem, just as we had done seven times before in the preceding two weeks. As I listened with my hand over my heart, I felt myself getting very emotional. Completely wrapped up in the moment, I thought again about my parents. I thought of the way they had led their lives, quietly proud, and what great Americans they were. My father passed away when I was a senior at West Point and my mom died in 1996, but I felt like this moment was more about them than me. It brought back that sense of perspective that makes you feel humbled by a moment that is so much bigger than you. I felt so grateful that I cried.

After the anthems played, the teams had a final three minutes to get ready. I used that three minutes to regain my composure. Being moved by "The Star-Spangled Banner" was a good thing—it felt great to experience emotion at that level. But I couldn't go into coaching the game distracted by that emotion. We had said that we were going to be ourselves. I had to settle down so that I could be myself in coaching my team against Spain. During that three minutes and throughout the Olympics, it helped tremendously to have Jim Boeheim by my side. Jim sat next to me in every game, and his presence gave me great confidence. Refocusing on the task at hand was much easier with my friend and one of the best coaches in the game right next to me.

Finally it was time for the opening tip. Pau Gasol and Dwight Howard went against each other for the jump ball, both falling to the floor in the process. We recovered the ball, and the first basket of the game was a LeBron James three-pointer. Pau Gasol answered on Spain's first possession with a three-point play of his own. It was a telling start.

Our team was whistled for several fouls early on and, exactly three and a half minutes into the game, Kobe and LeBron were in trouble with two each and our team trailing 13–9. This presented a challenge for us—obviously because two of our star players were forced to sit, but the disruption ran deeper than that. Our rotation was something we had consciously worked on over our five exhibitions and seven Olympic games. Now we were forced to change it in the championship game. Of our five starters, the two guys who typically remained in the game the longest had to come out, and we had to deviate from our established pattern. As we had throughout our time together, we had to adapt. We substituted Dwyane Wade and Deron Williams for Kobe and LeBron, who spent the rest of the first quarter on the bench, wrapped in towels to keep their muscles warm, dying to play.

Dwyane got to work right away. Ten seconds after getting into the game, he drove through the lane for a layup. Shortly afterward, he drove again and was fouled for a three-point play. Five points for Dwyane in forty-five seconds set the tone, telling both Spain and the fans, "Yes, two of our best players are stuck on the bench, but we are going to be just fine."

We finished the first quarter up 38–31, the most points we had scored in one quarter in the 2008 Olympics *and* the most we had given up. Two three-point plays by Chris Paul, the hustle of Chris Bosh, and the smart play of Tayshaun Prince helped get us through that first quarter. Dwyane Wade played magnificently on both ends of the court, finishing the quarter by hitting a three with ten seconds left and then stealing the ball, preventing Spain from scoring again. In those last six and a half minutes of the first quarter, we outscored Spain 29–18.

We put our starters back out on the court for the beginning of the second quarter. Fortunately, Kobe had been able to stay warm enough during his time on the bench to hit the first shot of the second quarter, a three-pointer. He also scored our team's next points on a breakaway dunk to put us up by 12, 43–31.

Everyone was hitting offensively: Carmelo with a three, Chris Paul with a beautiful three-quarter length of the court alley-oop to Kobe, LeBron with a strong drive to the bucket. Dwyane Wade reentered the game with 6:40 to play in the first half. With 5:12 left, he proceeded to get his third steal and drive full-court for a dunk. At the 4:50 mark, he hit another three. And with 4:04 left in the quarter, he drove and dished to LeBron James, who hit the open three, giving us a 14-point lead, the largest of the game. We were playing great offense. But Spain continued to fight back with their leader, Pau Gasol, the fearless play of Rudy Fernandez, and the gutsy performance of their seventeen-year-old guard, Ricky Rubio.

With about three minutes left, I put Tayshaun and Deron back in the game for Kobe and LeBron to ensure that they would not be called for their third fouls before halftime. Almost immediately,

Tayshaun made a terrific play, tapping in a missed layup to put us ahead by 11, 60–49.

There are statistics and then there are pressure statistics. One might look at the box score of the gold-medal game and see that Tayshaun Prince was three for three from the field, scoring six points and grabbing two offensive rebounds in eight minutes of play, and say, "That's not too bad." But stats don't tell you the crucial information of *when* those points were scored and *when* those rebounds were grabbed. Tayshaun didn't do those things when we had the game in hand, he did them when we needed them.

With 2:15 left in the half, Dwyane hit another three, his third. It was answered by a Fernandez three-pointer on the other end that kept Spain within nine. Over the last couple of minutes of the half, we traded points for points and fouls for fouls until the buzzer sounded and we went into the locker room, up by only eight points: 69–61. That's right—130 points had already been scored *at halftime.* Spain and the United States had combined to hit 41 of 65 shots from the field, an incredible 63 percent.

As I walked off the court toward the locker room, I thought about our defense. It had been the calling card of our team for the past three years and had failed us only once against Greece in 2006. "Was it failing us now?" I asked myself. In the Olympics, we had held teams to an average of less than 75 points a game. But Spain had already scored 61 in the first half. Still, the answer was no. Our defense was not failing us. The emotion of the game had lifted both teams to produce some tremendous offense, and we had still managed to earn the lead. Our defense was good; the offense was just spectacular.

Not only that, Spain was simply a very good team whose recent history in international play had them prepared to be at their best in this moment. Interestingly, the 1999 FIBA Junior (Under 19) World Championship in Lisbon saw the Spanish team defeat our US team in the gold-medal game, 94–87. That Spanish team featured five future 2008 Olympians. An eighteen-year-old Juan

Carlos Navarro had 27 points in that game, and a young Pau Gasol contributed seven points and five rebounds in seventeen minutes off the bench. Three years later, at the 2002 Senior World Championships in Indianapolis, Spain defeated the United States again in the fifth-place game, further boosting their confidence. In that game, Navarro contributed another 26 points and a more mature Pau Gasol started, giving his team 19 points and 10 rebounds in their six-point victory. In the 2004 Olympics, in which seven of the twelve 2008 Spanish Olympians participated, the Spain team went an impressive 5-0 in their pool before facing the 3-2 US team in the quarterfinals. Because we beat them in that quarterfinal game, led by 31 points from Tim Duncan, Spain found themselves in fifth place again. They were eager to meet us in the 2006 World Championship Finals but we did not make it there, having lost to Greece in the semifinals. Though we did not face one another in 2006, Spain proved itself a power by coming home with the gold medal, defeating Greece in the championship game by an impressive 23-point margin. Our 2008 matchup for the Olympic gold medal had been a long time coming.

Half of their Olympic roster had been playing together on the Spanish Senior National Team since 2002, and ten of the twelve had been together since at least 2006. This, plus their terrific guard play, gave them an offensive continuity that was difficult to disrupt. Our ability to defend became itself disrupted when LeBron and Kobe were saddled with their early fouls. In our substitution pattern, Dwyane Wade, Chris Paul, Deron Williams, and Chris Bosh would usually come into the game early to provide us with a boost on defense. Typically, Tayshaun was also asked to take on a more defensive-minded role. But with two of our top scorers on the bench three and a half minutes into the game, these players had to come in with a focus on putting points on the board. Then, when LeBron and Kobe came back into the game in the second quarter, they had to be cautious defensively so as not to pick up their third fouls. Basketball is a game of adjustments, and we had to adjust both to Spain's stellar offense and our team foul situation.

The halftime locker room was calm. There was no panic. No one spoke the words, "Come on, guys, this is the gold-medal game!" It didn't need to be said; we already recognized the moment. The atmosphere in that room was all business. Most of all, we couldn't wait for the fifteen minutes to be over so that we could get back out on the court. Kobe Bryant, who had been in more championship situations than the other players, did a lot of the talking. First, looking to Dwyane and Tayshaun, he thanked them for picking up the slack and keeping us in the game. Others joined in, briefly congratulating their teammates. I reminded my guys that in spite of our foul trouble, we had finished the half well and would begin the second half in good shape. Kobe concluded our halftime talk by saying, "We just saw their best. But they haven't seen our best yet." We left the locker room with our twenty most important minutes ahead of us.

Our starters took the court again at the beginning of the second half for another back-and-forth, ten-minute offensive battle. Right away, Spain cut the lead to six. Soon after, to four. We alternated being up six, then four, then six again for a few minutes before growing our lead. Carmelo had an excellent quarter for us, scoring seven points including a big three to put us up by 11 with under a minute left in the quarter. But the story for Spain in that ten minutes was the explosive play of Juan Carlos Navarro, who had looked so ready in warm-ups. In that ten-minute period, he had eight points on some tough shots, as well as a key assist in an alley-oop to Pau Gasol and a charge taken on a fast break drive by Deron Williams that could have expanded our lead back to 12. The final seconds of the quarter wound down and Navarro drove to the basket, putting the ball through the hoop as the buzzer sounded, cutting the US lead to single digits at 91–82.

Spain came out swinging in our final quarter of play, scoring seven straight points: four by their star Pau Gasol and a big-time three-pointer by Rudy Fernandez. With 8:23 left, it was a two-point game.

Timeout USA.

This was the most pressure our team had experienced in our three years together. It was at this moment that our character would be tested and ultimately revealed. The thought that kept running through my mind as the players came over to the bench was that this team *was* worthy of winning and that I trusted who we had become. There is a time to call a play and a time to let them play. As we huddled together before taking the court again, I told my team, "Just go out there and play."

Kobe Bryant would factor hugely in this moment. I believe he had gotten his birthday wish. He lives to be in big games, in championship situations. And this was even more than a championship, it was a gold medal. He had waited all summer, maybe all his life, for this moment. It was time to "set the Mamba loose."

The idea of this alter ego called the Black Mamba is something Kobe uses to psyche himself up, to elevate his game to another level when the pressure is on. When PBS's Charlie Rose asked me in an interview following the Olympics what it means to set the Mamba loose, I responded, "It means we're going to win!" My job as leader was just to make Kobe comfortable enough to follow his instincts in leading us through these final eight minutes.

On our first play out of the timeout, Kobe drove the ball into the lane with Spanish defenders all around him. I swear, he willed the ball through the hoop. USA up four.

Having received his third foul early in the quarter, LeBron was called for his fourth with 7:43 still left to play in the game. The question in coaching is: do you take him out to prevent him from getting his fifth and fouling out of the game? The answer in this moment was no. You leave LeBron in. He had been working for this moment for three years, and letting him play was my way of telling him that he had my complete trust.

On our next offensive possession, Kobe drove into the lane again. But this time, he found an open Deron Williams on the perimeter and passed it to him for a huge three-point shot. Deron nailed it. USA up seven.

After a miss by Spain, we regained possession and Kobe drove for a third time, dropping the ball into the waiting hands of Dwight Howard under the basket, who threw down a powerful dunk. Three Kobe Bryant drives with three different outcomes, all putting points on the board. USA up nine.

But Spain was not finished. At the other end, Rudy Fernandez sunk another three to put Spain back within six points with 6:20 to play.

In front of our bench, Deron dished it to Kobe again, who was open on the baseline. The three he hit with 6:02 to play completed a two-and-a-half-minute stretch in which the Mamba had scored or been responsible for 10 straight points. USA up nine.

Everyone on our bench was on their feet, supporting their teammates on the court. On the defensive end, Dwight Howard slapped away a missed shot, and as it headed out of bounds, LeBron chased it down, saving it in to Chris Paul and falling into the Spain bench. He came back into the play to receive a pass from Chris, and then went baseline but missed the driving layup. Somehow, he got his own rebound and put the ball through the hoop, completing a tremendous individual hustle possession. USA up 11.

Rudy Fernandez's incredibly athletic dunk on Spain's next possession was one of the highlights of the Olympics. It meant "We are definitely not going away," and the free throw he hit to complete the three-point play cut the lead to eight with five minutes to go.

Next, Dwight Howard was fouled on a layup attempt and hit one of two free throws. USA up nine.

On Spain's turn, Pau Gasol was fouled and converted on both of his free throw attempts, cutting the lead back to seven, 104–97.

After we were unable to score, Pau converted on a short jump shot to make the game even closer at 104–99.

Three minutes and twenty seconds away from someone having gold medals placed around their necks, Dwyane drove into the lane and kicked the ball out to Kobe behind the three-point line in a play that will go down as one of the most clutch in Olympic history. I know LeBron must have been thinking "game time" again when Kobe hit the three, was fouled, and sunk the free throw to complete a four-point play. The play meant that Rudy Fernandez would have to leave the game with his fifth foul. USA up nine.

But Spain was *still* not finished with their gold-medal effort. Navarro scored his 17th point on a runner in the lane that set the score at 108–101.

We did not convert on our end, and Spain's Carlos Jiminez hit his second three-pointer of the game to cut the lead back to four with 2:25 remaining.

Like Dwyane's assist and Kobe's four-point play from a minute and a half earlier, LeBron James's dish to Dwyane Wade is a play that will be remembered. Dwyane Wade is a big-game player. He had been that in 2006 when the Heat won the NBA Championship, and he had been that for his Marquette team when he took them to the Final Four in 2003. He was that for us on August 24, 2008. With 2:04 left, the gold-medal game's leading scorer put his 27th point on the board with a pressure-filled three that was nothing but net. USA up seven.

Timeout Spain.

With 1:52 left, Kobe committed his third foul, and Navarro went to the free throw line, where he hit the first. Missing the second, Spain was able to regain possession by knocking the ball out of bounds off of Chris Paul. They had one last chance, down six with 1:49 to play.

Spain missed on a three-point attempt, and LeBron came down with a powerful rebound to give us back possession.

There are certain short phrases in the language of basketball that can take on the meaning of entire paragraphs. With 1:31 left, up 111–105, the key basketball phrase that took on the most meaning for us was "time and score." At this point, in order to be sure we could come away with the win, our players had to be patient and realize that we were playing against all the numbers that appeared on the scoreboard but, most significant, those on the clock.

In a terrifically executed possession that played perfectly to the time and score, we used up twenty of the twenty-four seconds on the shot clock before Kobe drove and scored on a running layup. USA up eight.

When Spain couldn't score and we regained possession, we all knew that they would have to foul. At this point, what runs through a coach's mind is simply, "Don't let anything crazy happen." The players on the court have to be stronger with the ball because officials will allow more contact during these final minutes. You also have to be prepared to hit free throws. You have to act with the utmost poise. I felt great with Chris Paul as my point guard during these minutes. He played a flawless fourth quarter, hitting his two free throws after being fouled with forty-seven seconds left. USA up 10.

Scoring and cutting the lead to eight, Spain fouled Chris Paul again with 26.1 seconds on the clock. After putting together a truly extraordinary game, their team finally began to show frustration. They knew it was over, reacted, and were charged with a technical foul. Kobe made the two technical free throws and we called a timeout. Out of the timeout, Chris Paul hit one of his two free throws to make the score final: 118–107.

The last 26.1 seconds ticked off the clock with the crowd chanting, "USA! USA! USA!" and we became Olympic champions.

CONCLUSION:
OUR GOLDEN MOMENT

Take the time to celebrate your team's accomplishments.

I have said a lot in this book about how a leader has to set a tone, how sometimes moments are designed because you know that they're needed. But our golden moment could never have been scripted. Leaders aren't often surprised, especially when they have been in their business for a long time. But I never imagined the way I would feel. It was a time of pure joy, knowing we had accomplished our goal.

When we called the timeout with 26.1 seconds left on the clock in our gold-medal game, our players began to celebrate. I fought it at first, always believing that the celebration shouldn't begin until the final buzzer sounds.

I knelt to give my players some brief final instructions. As I began to stand, I felt several large hands on my head, messing up my hair. I think my hair had been an inside joke among the players and that many of them had looked forward to an opportunity to tousle it. Little by little, we were unable to suppress the genuine enthusiasm we all felt, and our "game faces" gave way to broad grins. With my hair all a mess, I hugged my leader Jason Kidd and thanked him for being the voice of experience we needed on our team. That man will leave behind an amazing legacy to the game of basketball and to the younger generation of point guards like Chris Paul and Deron Williams.

Next, I shared a hug with Dwyane Wade, the guy who was arguably the MVP of our 2008 summer. I will always remember what he said: "Thank you for believing in me." He was referring to the relationship we had during his 2007 recovery from knee and shoulder surgeries as well as our staff decision to include him on the Olympic roster. I want Dwyane to always know that it was easy to do. He believed in our team, he believed in representing his country, and he believed in making a commitment to both. He will stand out as a great example of how this kind of sincere mutual belief can pay off for everyone.

Kobe was standing directly behind us and likely realized that his hug would be next. As Dwyane and I pulled away from one another, Kobe bent down to pick up a bottle of water, presumably to quench his thirst. But when we hugged, I found out that the water was really for me. He poured it on my head, and as I turned away in surprise, he smacked me right on the rear end, laughing the entire time.

When asked later about the pressure and feeling of that fourth quarter, Kobe responded as only the Mamba would. "It was fun," he said. "Coming out of a timeout into a two-point game, look-ing around at the crowd and all the American flags waving. This is where we do it. This is what you dream about." You could tell by his post-game behavior that this may have been the most fun Kobe Bryant ever had.

As the timeout ended and Chris Paul went to the free throw line where he would score the game's final point, Tayshaun came and stood next to me, put his arm around my shoulder and said, "I told you we needed to have a serious practice yesterday." As usual, Tayshaun was right. We needed that serious practice to pre-pare us for a most serious test against Spain.

It was a test that I believe will go down as one of the great games in the history of international basketball. First, the fact that the winner received the gold medal puts it in the running. But, more than that, the game featured elite-level offensive performances by both squads. The combined score, 225, is the most points ever scored in an Olympic basketball game. Just to put it in perspective: if it had been a full, forty-eight-minute NBA game and both teams had continued to play at the same level, the score could have been 140–128.

And it was not merely the amount of points scored, but the accuracy with which each team shot the ball under gold-medal pressure. From two-point range, our team shot an incredible 26 for 37, 70 percent. And these were not just fast-break points. In our first game against Spain in pool play, we had scored 32 points on breaks. That's 32 free points. In this game, they played us differently, utilizing primarily a zone defense that forced us to work the ball. Even though they cut our break points in half, we found good shots on offense, just like we had practiced. And we were able to convert on the majority of them. For their part, Spain had shot very well, too: 53 percent from two-point territory and a terrific 47 percent from three.

In the team sport of basketball, a great game is about a lot of players playing great. It is not about an individual performance, though the 2008 gold-medal game saw some very good ones. Rudy Fernandez, who had averaged 12 points a game for Spain in the Olympics, had 22, shooting 5-9 from the three-point line. Pau Gasol had a predictably excellent performance with 21 points and six rebounds. And, after shooting 25 percent from the field in the Olympics, Juan Carlos Navarro shot 6 of 12 from two-point range and sunk six free throws to end up with 18 points. Every single Spanish player had stepped up his game that day.

Many are not aware of the level of basketball played that afternoon in Beijing. American viewers may have had trouble catching on because of the fact that the game aired at 2:30 in the morning on the East Coast. When they woke up the next morning and saw the 11-point margin of victory, they may have thought that Spain had given us a run but that we had handled it. Though the game was rebroadcast, I doubt people realized how close it had been down to the wire and maybe never took the time to investigate. In some ways, the true greatness of that game may be a secret shared by the die-hards who set their alarm clocks for 2:30 a.m. or were among those lucky people in attendance at Wukesong Arena on August 24, 2008.

As soon as the final buzzer sounded, indicating that three years of work had culminated in a gold medal, LeBron ran over to the sideline, jumped over the scorer's table and embraced Doug Collins. He was followed by the rest of our team, who had all been so moved by Doug's speech in Las Vegas. You could tell that LeBron had thought about this moment for a long time and that it was important enough to him that he had developed a mental checklist of all the things he wanted to do in his golden moment. One was to hug Doug Collins. "We all know his story," LeBron said afterward, "and what he went through with his Olympic experience, having a win basically taken from him. He's as important to this as we are. This is a gold for him also, not just us." We hope that Doug and the rest of the 1972 team feel that way. Our players certainly did.

When I made eye contact with Jerry Colangelo I didn't really know what to do, only this time it was for a much different reason than it had been after our loss to Greece in 2006. Of course, we hugged. We had accomplished our dream together. But the emotion I felt was so strong that I had to do something more. At a complete loss and in my moment of pure excitement, I kissed Jerry Colangelo on the cheek. It was a moment we and our families would joke about many times afterward. Jerry had brought out the best in me. I love that guy. He is one great American.

When I was able to make it over to the stands where my wife was watching the celebration, I leaned in and said to her, "You know how sometimes when you win, you just feel relieved?" Being at Duke for so long and having achieved some success there, sometimes the pressure to win feels overwhelming. So when you do win, what you feel is relief. You feel like, "Thank goodness we won because that's what was expected."

"Yes," she said. "You must feel very relieved, Michael."

"No, I don't feel that way. I don't feel relieved. I feel *exhilarated*."

I was not alone in this feeling of exhilaration. In my profession as a college coach, it is my job to turn boys into men. But in this celebratory Olympic moment, I found it extremely satisfying to see men become boys again, truly appreciating the joy of victory. In their lives and careers in sport, these men always have to project a tough and stoic image. But, in our golden moment, they couldn't help but show the childlike enthusiasm that they felt. And what made it even more beautiful was the fact that none of it was phony. It was real and pure. After respectfully shaking hands with the Spanish players, our guys huddled at midcourt and jumped up and down together before running excitedly back to our locker room to change into the blue and white hooded jackets and matching blue pants designed specifically for the occasion. The medal-stand uniform again united us with the larger American contingent. Every United States athlete was given one of these Nike warm-ups, and each one that medaled wore them as the symbols of their achievement were placed around their necks.

The feeling in the locker room was a wonderful combination of excitement and reflection. The players kept telling each other, "We've got to do this again," and "I'll be back in 2012 if you will." They wanted so badly to spray one another with champagne as they had seen so many championship teams do before, but this part of the celebration would have to wait until the bus ride back to the hotel because they had to look their best on the medal stand.

The coaches were just as excited but perhaps a bit more reflective than the players. We tried to appreciate the complete meaning of this moment—all we'd been through, how close we had become, how very different the feeling of this locker room was from the one after our loss in 2006. It was really neat the way the celebration seemed to come in waves as each member of our team entered the locker room: first the majority of the players, then the coaching staff, then Jerry Colangelo, then Kobe and Dwyane, who had just finished their sideline interview with NBC.

Amidst the excitement, I shared a great moment with Chris Bosh. He had been on an amazing journey of discovery that summer. I think it could change the course of his life and career. And I meant it when I said to him, "I want you to know that you have a friend for life."

"Coach," he replied, "you have one, too." We all did.

We reemerged from the locker room for the medal ceremony. First Argentina and then Spain received their bronze and silver medals. I loved watching as our twelve guys linked arms and stepped up in unison onto the gold-medal stand. Then, the emotion on their faces as they each received their medals. Chris Bosh took a visible deep breath before bending his head down as if to say, "This is finally it. I have to really feel this moment."

As the flags of our three nations were slowly raised, the American flag higher than the others, and as "The Star-Spangled Banner" was played, Jason turned to remind his teammates to place their hands over their hearts. A true leader till the end, Jason later said, "You can forget, in the emotion of winning, about the country and what that means. We did it the whole tournament, put our hands over our hearts. I didn't want any slippage because it wasn't over yet."

I have gone back and watched the footage of our fight song being played and our men standing shoulder to shoulder on the medal stand many times. I love watching Kobe singing along. I love the proud expression in Dwyane's teary eyes. And I really love the chiseled look of strength and dignity on LeBron's face. He was statuesque on that medal stand, a champion for the first time.

It was impossible not to notice the happiness of the Argentina and Spain teams receiving their medals. This was Spain's second medal performance in Olympic history and cemented their reputation as an international basketball power. Both the Spanish and Argentine teams were proud of their performances. And they should have been. After the ceremony, I made a point to go to the Argentina team and say to them, "I just want you to know that your team has the best spirit I have ever seen. And it was beautiful to see."

I think the other teams were impressed by our spirit, too. The Olympics are unique in that they provide nations with an opportunity, through sport, to both earn and give respect apart from all of the issues that cloud international relationships. In the past, basketball in the United States had promoted individualism. Now, we promoted team. Instead of garnering resentment, we garnered respect.

A lot of people are surprised to learn that Olympic coaches do not get medals. Only athletes are awarded this prestigious symbol. Following the medal presentation, our team gathered once more at center court to pose for pictures. It was there, in the midst of this team I had come to love, that I received my gold medal. In fact, I received twelve of them. One by one, the players placed their medals around my neck. It was a gesture I was not expecting. I knew then that the unity I had sought for this team had been achieved and it was felt by us all. What an incredible moment.

Jerry Colangelo and all three assistant coaches also had their turn to have the weight of the gold medal figuratively lifted from their shoulders and literally placed around their necks. We had done this together. Jerry was the architect and we built the team from his blueprint. This was their moment, too.

After the celebration on the court, it was time to prepare for our press conference. The protocol is for the coach and one or two players to meet with the press, but LeBron had told our team, "We're all going to the press conference together." And we did. The organizers had to scramble to make sure there was enough room for all twelve guys. But we had won this as a team and we were going to show up in front of the cameras as a team, too.

I think Kobe did a great job of summarizing the feeling when he said to the media, "What you saw today was a team. Everybody wants to talk about NBA players being selfish, being arrogant, being individuals. What you saw today was a team bonding together, facing adversity and coming out of here with a big win. . . . It's an unbelievable feeling to win a gold medal for your country. I can't begin to describe to you the feeling that we all feel right now."

Jason added to Kobe's sentiment: "We had one ego and that is the team ego. We wanted to play as a team. . . . With all the great players and the egos we became one ego, a team ego, and that growth was a beautiful thing to see."

And Deron reflected on what the win meant for him when he said, "It's been a great experience for me, a lifetime experience. Something I'm going to cherish the rest of my life. . . . I have stories to tell my kids. It's kind of surreal right now to think that I'm an Olympic champion. . . . [This is] number one on my list. . . . This is for your country . . . it's for a whole nation of people back home supporting us, for our troops overseas fighting for us. This is for everybody."

Even in our culminating, celebratory moment as a team, the players recognized both the context and perspective surrounding our victory. We showed the humility that comes with being a part of something much bigger than you. And we shared it all with our families, friends, and a nation of fans. The next morning's *USA Today* sports section headline read, "Winning with Class" and began, "Even the joyous scene which followed the U.S. men's basketball team's thrilling 118–107 gold-medal victory against Spain was as selfless as the play which had defined [the Americans'] Olympic performance. They gathered in a circle, arms draped around each other's shoulders. On the podium, they stood arm in arm. Posing for pictures, they put all their medals around Coach Mike Krzyzewski's neck and they mussed his mostly unmovable hair."

Sally Jenkins's article in the *Washington Post*, titled "Salvation's Army," also described the post-game celebration beautifully: "Kobe Bryant saluted. Carmelo Anthony wrapped an American flag around his waist like a towel. They kissed their gold medals, and studied them like children looking at new pennies, and held up roses. . . . There was something irresistibly affecting about such very large and serious-faced men jumping around so giddily, after beating such a smart and dogged team in Spain."

After twenty-four hours of travel home from China, the Polish Griswalds finally arrived at Raleigh-Durham International Airport. I felt the benefits of my home support system again as we were met by my staff and some of the many fans who had cheered us on. There were red, white, and blue balloons everywhere and a large American flag hanging behind a podium. When I stepped up to speak I said, "It's good to be home." In discussing my experience, I told the group, "You don't realize how proud you are to be an American until you're in a setting like the Olympics. But it's so good now to just be the Duke coach." I added, "I'm anxious to see my team." I would have that opportunity even sooner than I expected.

My family of thirteen, along with Chris and Kim Collins, and Steve Wojciechowski, all boarded a minibus to take us to our respective homes—sixteen people and three times as many bags. We were all exhausted. My grandchildren fell asleep in their seats. My daughters looked like they might as well. But as we drove past the Duke campus, those of us still awake smiled to see that a new sign was hanging over the street, again with the Duke and USA Basketball symbols. This one read, "Congratulations Coach K! 2008 Men's Basketball Olympic Gold Medal." For a couple of weeks I was able to see this on my way to and from work and feel good about both the team I had been on and the one to which I had come home.

After having been away for forty days, it felt good when the bus finally made the turn into my driveway. As we made our way slowly up the long drive, I could see that there was a group of people waiting outside our front door. As we came closer, I realized that it was my entire Duke team, including the staff and managers who had kept things running so smoothly while I had been gone. When I got off the bus, they all gave Chris, Wojo, and me hugs of congratulations. I had just returned from the greatest experience of my coaching career, but it was really nice to be back to what was familiar and to know that these were the young men who would be with me as I embarked on my twenty-ninth season at Duke. Maybe there was even a future Olympian in that group.

Later that night I got a call from Shane Battier, who had played with the National Team in 2006. He wanted to pass on his congratulations to the team.

I said to him, "Thank you for the role that you played."

"I played a small role," he conceded. His comment was intended to deflect the attention from what he had contributed, but I heard so much more. I heard recognition that he had, indeed, played a role in our Olympic victory, and it made me feel good knowing that twenty-one other guys who had been in our pool of thirty-three, the players and coaches who had been a part of the Select Team, and countless players, coaches, and staff who had been a part of USA Basketball over the years could feel that way, too. Hopefully this feeling would last, meaning that we not only accomplished our goal of winning the gold but also planted the seeds for the future of the program.

After our hard-fought victory over Spain, some questioned why we had not won by more, seeing it as a chink in our armor. I see it as exactly the opposite. Both the Spain and Argentina games had served as validation of our three years of work, confirming that the system needed to change and that we had done what was necessary to give us a chance of winning. The world was indeed much improved, and no matter how talented the personnel we put on the floor, we can no longer succeed without embracing the notion of team. There is no doubt in my mind that we could have lost both those games had we not together formed relationships, established standards, and engaged in some honest self-assessment.

For me, Spain's performance in that game provided the perfect ending to our fairy tale. The hard-fought victory was more than a validation of our learning of the language and our preparation; it was a validation of the relationships that we had built with one another. People could see that the brotherhood was real. As Kobe later phrased it, "You could see that the system worked. The process had built a team with camaraderie and chemistry. We were tested and we faced adversity and we were able to dig deep and work together to pull out that game." Our team character had been revealed, and it was something of which we could all be most proud.

From now on when I am asked how to build a team, I know exactly the story I will tell. It will be about the opportunity that I had to coach the USA Basketball Men's Senior National Team for three years. I will tell about the quantity and quality of the time that we spent together, the way we faced challenges and grew through competition, and the amazing feeling of accomplishment we all experienced when, together, we achieved our ultimate goal.

I will remind people that there is no formula, no recipe, no easy step-by-step process. My story can serve only as a guide. Any advice I offer may give you direction, but it will not make it easy. Team building is hard work. Take the time to choose your people, understand context, gain perspective, form relationships, develop a support system, establish standards, cultivate leadership, adapt internally, learn the language, practice, self-assess, and get motivated. If you personalize these times for your team and experience your own team-building moments, you will have the opportunity at game time to discover who you have become. Then, don't forget to celebrate. In celebration, you relive your moments together and your hard work is validated and rewarded by the way you feel. There is no better feeling than having been a part of a world-class team.

USA BASKETBALL MEN'S SENIOR NATIONAL TEAM 2006–2008 ROSTER

Name	Height	Weight	Date of Birth	Current Team/ College or High School
Carmelo Anthony	6-8	230	5/29/84	Denver Nuggets/Syracuse
Gilbert Arenas	6-4	210	1/06/82	Washington Wizards/Arizona
Shane Battier	6-8	220	9/09/78	Houston Rockets/Duke
Chauncey Billups	6-3	202	9/25/76	Denver Nuggets/Colorado
Carlos Boozer	6-9	266	11/20/81	Utah Jazz/Duke
Chris Bosh	6-10	230	3/24/84	Toronto Raptors/Georgia Tech
Bruce Bowen	6-7	200	6/14/71	San Antonio Spurs/California State Fullerton
Elton Brand	6-8	254	3/11/79	Philadelphia 76ers/Duke
Kobe Bryant	6-6	205	8/23/78	Los Angeles Lakers/Lower Marion High School (PA)
Tyson Chandler	7-1	225	10/02/82	New Orleans Hornets/Dominguez High School (CA)
Nick Collison	6-10	255	10/26/80	Oklahoma City Thunder/Kansas
Kevin Durant	6-9	220	9/29/88	Oklahoma City Thunder/Texas
Kirk Hinrich	6-3	190	1/02/81	Chicago Bulls/Kansas
Dwight Howard	6-11	265	12/08/85	Orlando Magic/Southwest Atlanta Christian Academy (GA)
LeBron James	6-8	250	12/30/84	Cleveland Cavaliers/St. Vincent–St. Mary High School (OH)
Antawn Jamison	6-9	235	6/12/76	Washington Wizards/North Carolina
Joe Johnson	6-7	230	6/29/81	Atlanta Hawks/Arkansas

Jason Kidd	6-4	210	3/23/73	Dallas Mavericks/California
Shawn Marion	6-7	228	5/07/78	Miami Heat/University of Nevada—Las Vegas
Brad Miller	7-0	261	4/12/76	Sacramento Kings/Purdue
Mike Miller	6-8	218	2/19/80	Minnesota Timberwolves/Florida
Adam Morrison	6-8	205	7/19/84	Charlotte Bobcats/Gonzaga
Greg Oden	6-10	250	1/22/88	Portland Trail Blazers/Ohio State
Lamar Odom	6-10	230	11/06/79	Los Angeles Lakers/Rhode Island
Chris Paul	6-0	175	5/06/85	New Orleans Hornets/Wake Forest
Paul Pierce	6-6	230	10/13/77	Boston Celtics/Kansas
Tayshaun Prince	6-9	215	2/28/80	Detroit Pistons/Kentucky
Michael Redd	6-6	215	8/24/79	Milwaukee Bucks/Ohio State
JJ Redick	6-4	190	6/24/84	Orlando Magic/Duke
Luke Ridnour	6-1	167	2/13/81	Milwaukee Bucks/Oregon
Amare Stoudemire	6-10	240	11/16/82	Phoenix Suns/Cypress Creek High School (FL)
Dwyane Wade	6-4	216	1/17/82	Miami Heat/Marquette
Deron Williams	6-3	205	7/26/84	Utah Jazz/Illinois

Managing Director: Jerry Colangelo

Head Coach: Mike Krzyzewski, Duke University

Assistant Coach: Jim Boeheim, Syracuse University

Assistant Coach: Mike D'Antoni, New York Knicks

Assistant Coach: Nate McMillan, Portland Trail Blazers

Team Physician: Sheldon Burns, Minnesota Timberwolves

Athletic Trainer: Keith Jones, Houston Rockets

Athletic Trainer: Casey Smith, Dallas Mavericks

Director of Scouting: Rudy Tomjanovich

Director of Player Personnel: Johnny Dawkins, Stanford University

Director of International Player Personnel: Tony Ronzone, Detroit Pistons

2006 World Championship Team Roster

- #15 Carmelo Anthony
- #8 Shane Battier
- #11 Chris Bosh
- #14 Elton Brand
- #5 Kirk Hinrich
- #12 Dwight Howard
- #6 LeBron James
- #7 Antawn Jamison
- #4 Joe Johnson
- #13 Brad Miller
- #10 Chris Paul
- #9 Dwyane Wade

2007 FIBA Americas Championship Team Roster

- #15 Carmelo Anthony
- #4 Chauncey Billups
- #10 Kobe Bryant
- #14 Tyson Chandler
- #11 Dwight Howard
- #6 LeBron James
- #5 Jason Kidd
- #13 Mike Miller
- #9 Tayshaun Prince
- #8 Michael Redd
- #12 Amare Stoudemire
- #7 Deron Williams

2008 Olympic Team Roster

- #15 Carmelo Anthony
- #4 Carlos Boozer
- #12 Chris Bosh
- #10 Kobe Bryant
- #11 Dwight Howard
- #6 LeBron James
- #5 Jason Kidd
- #13 Chris Paul
- #14 Tayshaun Prince
- #8 Michael Redd
- #9 Dwyane Wade
- #7 Deron Williams

ACKNOWLEDGMENTS

There are two groups of people that need to be recognized for the roles that they played in this project. First, there are those whose assistance facilitated the actual writing and production of the book. And second, there are those who made the experience itself possible. Without their efforts, the National Team story would not be one so worthy of telling.

Specifically related to the book, I would like to thank David Falk and Mike Cragg for their help in getting the project off the ground. Eric Lautenbach from Nike, George Land from NBA Entertainment, and Craig Miller from USA Basketball made themselves consistently available to answer our many questions and provide us with requested research material. Chris Spatola, Steve Wojciechowski, and Chris Collins gave generously of their time, providing some of the book's best stories and helping to fill in specifics. Our editor, Rick Wolff, was, as always, a constant source of ideas and constructive feedback. His editing expertise made a great difference, as did the efforts of Mark Steven Long, Mari Okuda, and Tracy Martin. Most of all, Sean Ford gave us the gift of his incredible memory, retelling moments I may have forgotten and recalling details that turned good stories into great ones. Sean was almost as important to this book as he was to the National Team. And that's saying a lot.

I cannot write an acknowledgments section to this book without expressing my gratitude to Jerry Colangelo, who trusted me to become his partner in this endeavor and, in the process, became my great friend. Thank you also to my USAB coaching staff—Jim Boeheim, Mike D'Antoni, and Nate McMillan—who offered their time and expertise to our worthy goal. Additionally, I would like to express my gratitude to Duke Athletic Director Kevin White and my entire Duke family, who were encouraging throughout.

Many thanks to my friends at Nike, who provided unwavering support for USA Basketball and helped us broadcast our message. Phil Knight, George Raveling, Eric Lautenbach, Michael Jackson, and Lynn Merritt were valued members of our team.

And, of course, to the thirty-three professional players who comprised America's National Team. You all made your country and your colleagues in the sport of basketball very proud. It is your efforts and attitude that set the gold standard for the future of our sport and for anyone interested in learning what it takes to build a world-class team from a group of very talented individuals.

And finally, there is one person who belongs in both of these classes and a class all her own: my wife, Mickie. In addition to being there with me every step of the National Team journey, she is a brilliant editor who lent numerous hours and many of her own words to the project. She made this book better, just as she has always made me better.

INDEX